THE MOUNTAIN BAKER

the
MOUNTAIN
BAKER

MIMI COUNCIL & KIMMY FASANI

100 High-Altitude Recipes
for Every Occasion

THE COUNTRYMAN PRESS
A division of W. W. Norton & Company
Independent Publishers Since 1923

For information about permission to reproduce
selections from this book, write to Permissions,
The Countryman Press, 500 Fifth Avenue,
New York, NY 10110

For information about special discounts for bulk
purchases, please contact W. W. Norton Special Sales
at specialsales@wwnorton.com or 800-233-4830

Manufacturing by Toppan LeeFung
Book design by Mia Johnson
Production manager: Devon Zahn

The Countryman Press
www.countrymanpress.com

A division of W. W. Norton & Company, Inc.
500 Fifth Avenue, New York, NY 10110
www.wwnorton.com

978-1-68268-415-3

10 9 8 7 6 5 4 3 2 1

For our husbands,
who love to play outside and eat
whatever we put in front of them.

CONTENTS

31
BREADS & PASTRIES

79
MADE FOR ADVENTURE

53
EATS

101
APRÈS

125
REFRESHMENTS

147
HEARTY EATS

171
COOKIES & BARS

199
CAKES & PIES

BAKING UP A STORM

Living in a small mountain town was never something I saw myself doing. I am from Chicago and always considered myself a city girl. I grew up taking the train, shopping on Michigan Avenue, and locking my doors at night. But while all my friends took vacations to tropical places during winter, coming back with a tan, the only tan I got was a goggle tan. Where did I go? West. To even colder destinations with big mountains and lots of snow. Every year we spent our vacations skiing at resorts like Steamboat, Crested Butte, and Park City. We even named our golden retriever Brighton, after the ski resort in Utah. The things I really enjoyed about our ski trips were the mountain life-style, food, and mind-set.

My food obsession began at Montessori preschool. While all the other girls were playing with dolls I was in the "kitchen." We were taught how to make mini pizzas in a toaster oven with English muffins, tomato sauce, and shredded cheese. After I learned I could bake and eat pizza at school, I did it every chance I could get. I even offered to make them for other students, kids I wasn't even friends with. When I felt I had perfected the English Muffin Pizza, I showed off my skills to my parents. I learned that I liked making food for others, though I was completely unaware at the time that my life would be consumed with it. I cherished those English muffin pizzas so much that I even created a grown-up version, Pizza Bread (page 153).

Because I was fascinated by food, of course I set my eyes on a lavender Easy Bake Oven. I was so excited about that oven, and equally disappointed when I baked whatever it was you were supposed to bake inside it. I couldn't figure out how the food looked so good on TV and tasted so bad in real life. I believe this is part of what made me the type of baker who cares more about ingredients than presentation. Needless to say, I ditched my Easy Bake Oven after that and graduated to a real oven. I was baking cookies, brownies, and cakes all on my own. This was the time in my preteen years when I was uprooted from my life and plopped into a small town in the bottom left of the mitten—in Michigan.

One of the perks of living in Michigan was a ski hill, located just 15 minutes from our house. Before I knew it, I was competing in snowboard contests and traveling all over the country. I attended a snowboard academy in Southern Vermont, and I graduated high school early so that I could move to a small ski town in the eastern side of the

Sierra Nevada mountains. And in the middle of that crazy time, I met a girl named Kimmy Fasani. I had no idea that our paths would cross again.

Food didn't take a back seat to snow-boarding; it was just more of a partner in crime. But a silent partner that never took any credit. It was there when I needed it, and it made my experiences that much better. I'd wake up in our winter cabin in Harbor Springs, Michigan, to the smell of my dad cooking Bagel French Toast (page 67). The smell always made its way up the wood pan-eled staircase to the two bedrooms and one bathroom my family of five shared. When I got downstairs, there would be a makeshift sign hanging on the kitchen cabinet door that read, DAD'S DINER. French toast wasn't the only thing on the menu. Ham & Cheese Omelets (page 72) and Honey Graham Pan-cakes (page 63) will forever remind me of crisp winter mornings at our ski house.

It was no surprise to my family when I moved cross country to Mammoth Lakes, California. I was 17 years old when I traded in my parent's house for a ski shack that was within walking distance to a gondola. I

missed my parent's fully stocked kitchen with all the tools and things I liked for baking, but I made do. I learned how to budget my gro-cery money so I could buy baking supplies. And I learned how to bake at high altitude out of pure necessity, with the old-fashioned trial-and-error method.

I then spent some time away from the mountains and fell even more in love with baking. Upon my return to Mammoth, I real-ized what I should really be doing with my life. That's when I ran into Kimmy Fasani. It seemed like fate that two old friends were standing in the bakery section of the market so I told her my plans to open an organic bake shop. Never did I think that our conversation would change my life forever. Kimmy and her husband, Chris Benchetler, gave me the extra boost of capital I needed to open Dessert'D Organic Bake Shop.

The Benchetlers have become so much more than just investors and partners; I now consider them family. Kimmy is always there, cooking food for me after I've spent 15 hours in the bake shop and haven't had a chance for a real meal. I've been known to come into her house, ravenous from working, and inhale Sweet Potato Fries (page 123). Our combined love of the outdoors and baking has made Dessert'D Organic Bake Shop what it is today. Most of my days are spent baking in a small but quaint kitchen at Dessert'D Organic Bake Shop's brick-and-mortar loca-tion in our small mountain town. If I'm not baking for the day-to-day operations, I am creating new and interesting recipes, which has become my absolute favorite part of my job. Being creative and experimenting with new desserts and flavors is how I got here, and I am so thankful that most days I am still doing exactly that.

COOKING UP ADVENTURE

The mountains are more than a destination for me. They run deep in my veins and have ultimately shaped my life into what it has become, that of a professional snowboarder and food lover. The countless days I have spent wandering among towering mountain peaks have shown me how rewarding spending time in nature can be for the mind and the body. Over time I have learned how important good food is in fueling both of these, as well as my adventures.

I was born and raised in Truckee, California, a small town tucked into the Sierra Nevada mountains about 15 minutes from Lake Tahoe. My earliest memories are that of exploring and playing in the rugged high elevation terrain that was my home. My mom was an outdoor enthusiast, and I spent my early childhood on her back in a backpack as she hiked the trails around the lake. She was a clever cook and always packed the best snacks, like Baked Breakfast Cups (page 59) and granola to keep me happy and moving.

As the seasons changed so did our adventures. By the time I was 22 months old my mom had me on skis. By five years old I was on a ski race team, and it took me a mere four years to convince my mom to let me snowboard. On my ninth Christmas, she surprised

me with the snowboard of my dreams; it was lightly used and from a ski swap. My weekends consisted of ski races in the morning, a lunchtime treat of Sweet Potato Fries (page 123) that were reserved only for race days, and snowboarding until the mountain closed.

While I spent most of my time out on the mountain, I remember being so excited to come home to big bowls of Mom's homemade Hearty Winter Stew (page 157), which she always paired with her freshly baked Mountain Bread (page 33). Making food together was a special time for us, and her focus was always to show me how to make quick and easy, high-quality meals. Many nights we prepped vegetables together so she could throw everything in the slow cooker before we left in the morning. She made frequent comments about why cooking and baking at high altitude required recipes to be altered, but I didn't fully appreciate her insights until I was living on my own.

I entered my first snowboard contest and made it to USASA Nationals the same year. And after a lucky streak of a few podium finishes for Slopestyle, I was motivated and passionate about making snowboarding my career. When I graduated high school I moved to Mammoth Lakes, California. My mom was incredibly supportive, and she encouraged

me to chase my dreams, but she advised me to have a backup plan just in case. So I signed up for school at the community college and got a job at a local restaurant to help pay for my snowboarding pursuits. My love for food and cooking came flooding into my life while working at that restaurant. Being constantly surrounded by food inspired me to cook at home. Now that I lived at 8,000 feet above sea level, I realized why all my mom's recipes had modifications; living at altitude was a science when it came to baking.

My love of desserts grew simultaneously with my love of cooking food in general. This passion is actually what led me to meet my husband, professional big mountain skier Chris Benchetler, who at the time was a young and ambitious rising star in freestyle skiing. I frequently got my sweet tooth fix at the local ice cream shop where he worked. As soon as we began dating, his mom, Kathy, took me under her wing and shared her love of cooking with me. Since Chris lived at home, I spent the majority of my time at the Benchetlers'. Kathy is a vegetarian, and she would prepare delicious vegetable dishes all the time. Some of my favorites made their way into this book,

like Baked Brussels Sprouts with Sweet Chili Sauce (page 112) and Lemon Tahini Kale Chips (page 116).

As I transitioned from being a competitive snowboarder to a big mountain backcountry rider, the food I was eating changed accordingly. I needed high-quality, long-lasting meals and snacks that would give me enough energy to maintain the long, 12 to 14 hour days I spent hiking around and riding in the highest snow-covered mountains. I dabbled with eating gluten-free, vegan, vegetarian, and raw. Ultimately, I learned that moderation was key for me to embrace a well-balanced diet. I realized the importance of having a breakfast that was power-packed with nutrients, like my famous Protein Waffles (page 71), which gave me plenty of sustainable energy during a day well spent in the outdoors. I also got creative with foods like the First Chair Granola (page 55), which was great as a quick morning bowl of cereal or as a packable snack that I could bring with me into the mountains.

Chris and I met because of our mutual love of sweets, and desserts are especially dear to us. So when the opportunity came to us to be involved with Mimi and Dessert'D Organic Bake Shop, we decided that being part of something like this in our local community was a no-brainer. We had always wanted to give something back to the small town that had given us so much. Food has always been a way for me to give back to the people I love, and this was putting that love on a bigger scale. Over the years my appreciation for living at high altitude has made me really aware that not all recipes are created equal, and by passing down my favorite recipes I hope to inspire others to cook up adventures wherever they are.

INTRODUCTION

When the opportunity for this book came to me, I felt a strong urge to ask my friend and partner, Kimmy Fasani, to write it with me. We started Dessert'D Organic Bake Shop together, and I knew this book wouldn't be complete without her. After all, Kimmy is the "Mountain" and I am the "Baker."

When I first came to Mammoth as a teenager, I quickly realized I couldn't bake my favorite cookie recipe—and I knew I had to fix that. So I spent a lot of time testing and crafting recipes that could be baked at high altitude, which is considered 5,000 feet and above. As I experimented, I graduated from cookies to cakes and beyond. Most of the time, regardless of the baked good, I found myself ditching my old recipes and starting from scratch. While that was necessary in order to develop recipes that worked, it also meant I was gaining all these new and amazing recipes. Looking back, I realize that living at an altitude of 8,000 feet didn't mean I had to give up baking some of my favorite desserts. It just meant I had to create recipes for them in a different way.

When Dessert'D opened in September 2011, I was the only employee. Kimmy's investment was purely financial, as she was at the top of her professional snowboarding career at the time. While Kimmy was off making history, chasing winter, and winning the coveted award of Women's Rider of the Year, I was working in the bake shop. I spent all day there doing everything from baking cookies, washing dishes, and serving customers, to managing our social media, website, and more; making it the success that it is today. Years of 15-hour days, an insane amount of pies, and thousands of cookies later, I am finally able to breathe and take a step back. All the blood, sweat, and tears that went into the bake shop were warranted. I now have a manager, Thea Zobel, who is one of our new partners at Dessert'D. I have a small staff of amazing people who I can count on. And we're selling franchises, so we will have more Dessert'D Organic Bake Shop locations.

It wasn't until these things took shape that I had time to think about sharing my recipes and high-altitude baking knowledge. When I started our mountain bake shop, I had unknowingly set out on a mission to create recipes that would work for everyone. Now, in this book, we are finally sharing some of our most cherished desserts, snacks, and meals. For us, loving the mountains and baking go hand in hand. You shouldn't have to choose between one and the other. And now you don't have to! Bake up a storm in any mountain town with confidence and with recipes that are meant for your lifestyle. And if you're not in the mountains now, go ahead and make these recipes and be transported into a state of mountain bliss. Just know you can bring this book with you *anywhere* and count on our recipes to work, no matter where you call home. —MIMI

HIGH-ALTITUDE
COOKING & BAKING

Baking and cooking both require different methods at high altitude. The main difference to remember is that baking will be a little bit faster and cooking will take a little bit longer.

COOKING

Cooking isn't nearly as precise as baking, and that's part of what we love about it. But be aware of some small differences at higher altitudes. The first noticeable difference is the change in boiling point. At sea level, water boils at 212°F. But at an altitude of 8,000 feet, water actually boils at 195°F. This means that your water will reach its boiling point faster at high altitude than at sea level because it boils at a lower temperature. However, because it boils at a lower temperature, the temperature of the boil isn't as hot. This means that cooking over a stovetop will result in slightly longer cook times at higher altitudes.

The recipes in this book for cooking are the same for high altitude and sea level. Unlike baking, we can give ranges and visual cues in cooking to indicate when your food is done or when it's ready for the next step. It's fairly easy to detect those cues when you're cooking on the stovetop versus when something is hidden inside an oven. While there may be slight variations of a few minutes from sea level to high altitude, we think that it's such a small difference that the recipes can be followed the same way. For example, if you're boiling the noodles for our Baked Mac 'N' Cheese (page 158), the cook time may be a little bit longer than what the box states because the water is boiling at a lower temperature. So make sure to test that your noodles are done.

BAKING

Baking is a little more technical than cooking, which is why it requires exact measurements and exact timing. High-altitude baking is usually faster than baking at sea level. Part of us loves this, because it means we can make fresh cookies quicker. But part of us is also aware that there are some gotchas to watch out for. Number one: A shorter baking time means baked goods rise faster at altitude. But because they rise faster, those baked goods are also at risk of falling. Have you ever baked a cake at high altitude, checked it partway through, saw that it looked great, and then found it sunk by the time you removed it from the oven? Yes, we've been there too—you can come back from that!

Another common mistake is burning. Blackened cookies are no fun, so keep in mind that the speed of high-altitude baking means sea-level bake times won't work. If you're following a recipe for sea level when baking in the mountains, you can easily burn your cookies.

You should also be aware of the lower humidity at high altitudes. This can affect baking if your recipe is not developed for high altitude. Because of the lower humidity, baked goods dry out faster. Most baked goods are made up of sugar, and sugar contains a high amount of moisture. Because water boils at a lower temperature, that moisture evaporates faster than the time it takes to finish baking. This can wreak havoc on a recipe developed at sea level. Too little moisture in a baked good can be an additional cause of sunken desserts, making fallen cakes and flat cookies a common trend at high altitude.

The last major difference about baking at high altitude has to do with storing your finished treats. As mentioned above, the higher you are in altitude, the dryer it is. If you don't properly store desserts, the dry air can ruin them in a matter of hours. We give specific instructions in this book for storing all baked goods when you're at altitude. But, generally, if you are in the mountains, a simple rule of thumb is if the dessert is soft, chewy, moist, or cakey, it needs to be stored in an airtight container to retain its moisture. This will conserve its soft texture. Conversely, for a dessert that is crispy or crunchy, then the dry mountain air is the perfect climate for it, and it can be left out on the counter, buffet, or table all day long with no problems.

We'll put it bluntly: Sea-level baking recipes are not made for high altitude. But on the plus side, if a recipe is developed at high altitude, then there's no problem bringing it down to sea level with just a minor adjustment (if at all) to the baking time. Like with boiling water, an item can take just a little bit longer in the oven at sea level.

All the recipes in our book are written to be made at high altitude, and you'll find "Sea Level" notes for making simple adjustments at sea level. No more fallen cakes, no more flat cookies, no more stress—just beautiful and delicious desserts, dinners, and snacks, no matter where you live.

KITCHEN GEAR

When you're outside in the mountains it is important to have the right gear. It can save your life, or just take your day from struggling to soaring. Cooking and baking are similar to a day outside in the mountains in that you can have an amazing experience or a frustrating one. Having the right tools will make your experience that much more enjoyable. Here are some common kitchen tools we recommend you use to create the recipes in this book.

BAKING DISHES: We use a couple of differently sized baking dishes for the recipes in this book, but we predominantly use 9-by-13-inch rectangles and 9-by-9-inch squares. It's important to have the right size dishes so that the baking times are accurate for each recipe. Both are great sizes to have on hand.

BAKING SHEETS: 13-by-18-inch baking sheets are standard size for home baking. These are super important to keep in your kitchen, and not just for baking sweets! Sweet Potato Fries (page 123) use baking sheets, and you're going to want to make those. We recommend using aluminum baking sheets for the best results. Other baking sheets could yield different results in the oven.

CAKE PANS: We call for a couple types of round cake pans for the recipes in the book: 6-inch and 9-inch. Only one 9-inch cake pan and three 6-inch cake pans are needed. We also use a loaf cake pan that is 9-by-5 inches, and it can be aluminum or ceramic. Lastly, we use a 9-inch Bundt pan that holds 8 to 10 cups. We prefer silicone Bundt pans because they allow the cake to come out easily and there's absolutely no worry! As soon as it's cooled, you just peel off the pan and you have a perfect Bundt cake. Aluminum is also an option, but make sure to grease and flour an aluminum pan very well in order to have a perfect-looking cake.

CAST-IRON SKILLET: We use a 10-inch cast-iron skillet for a few recipes, like the Bacon Chocolate Chip Cookie Skillet (page 181). It's really important that the skillet be cast iron so it can go inside the oven and bake evenly. A cast-iron skillet is an amazing tool to have for your kitchen; not only can you cook over the stovetop, but you can also bake with it!

DIGITAL SCALE: At Dessert'D we use a digital scale to weigh everything. For baking, we can't stress enough how important it is to weigh your ingredients. All you need is an inexpensive digital scale that can fit inside a kitchen drawer. It's a small tool that can make a big difference in your baked goods. Measuring inaccurately is a common mistake in baking, and if you use a scale, your time will be well spent honing your baking skills instead. This is less important for cooking, as it isn't as much of a science as baking. If you want to ditch your scale for cooking, we fully support that!

DIGITAL THERMOMETER: A digital thermometer is an essential kitchen tool. It can be used to make so many things, including Old-Fashioned Hot Cocoa (page 128).

DUTCH OVENS: A Dutch oven really helps to make things like Mountain Bread (page 33), because heat is locked inside in a way that creates a perfect crust. We prefer to use a 2.75-quart size. The Dutch oven is unique in its many benefits to baking bread: It helps with the loaf volume and the crust, and it keeps the loaf from burning before the inside is done baking. If you don't have a Dutch oven, you can create a foil tent for each loaf while baking on a sheet pan. This tent will keep the loaf from burning.

FOOD PROCESSOR: A food processor is necessary to make some of the recipes in this book, such as Personal Cauliflower Pizzas (page 154) and Honey Graham Pancakes (page 63). It's important to have this tool for the recipes that call for it. It doesn't have to be very large—even a 3-cup food processor will work just fine.

KNIVES: Make sure to have a good set of knives, from a chef's knife to a serrated knife. Good knives are essential for cutting delicate creations like Rosemary Parmesan Biscotti (page 104), as the savory biscotti is very fragile. You should also sharpen your knives regularly so they do their job and you get nice clean cuts.

MANDOLINE: A mandoline might seem like a fancy kitchen tool, but don't be intimidated. It's really just a cutting machine that does all the work for you! To make recipes like Zucchini Chips & Hummus (page 120) and Potato Chips & Onion Dip (page 119), this essential tool ensures you get the right size and slice for the cooking time. It's a great investment for your kitchen. Just make sure that your mandoline has sizes in inches, as we've found that some just have numbers with no corresponding sizes. Having the correct thickness is crucial to baking times.

MEASURING CUPS AND SPOONS: You should have a set of measuring cups and spoons on hand. When using them, be sure to measure to the brim of each. We prefer to use measuring cups over a liquid measuring cup because the actual cups are more accurate. If you aren't looking at the liquid measuring cup exactly straight on, the measurement can be off.

MIXING BOWLS: Have a good set of mixing bowls in various sizes. We prefer glass or metal, but whatever you like best will do just fine. Just make sure to use heatproof bowls when melting chocolate, such as in the Cookies 'N' Cream Biscotti (page 190).

MUFFIN TINS AND LINERS: Standard size muffin tins are needed to bake the muffins in this book's recipes. These are the same size as cupcake tins and liners, so if you have those, you're all set.

PARCHMENT PAPER: Parchment paper is a key tool to have in your kitchen. We prefer to use the nonbleached, natural parchment paper, which can be reused multiple times for cookies. Not only does it make baking cookies, biscotti, and bars easier, it's crucial for making our Potato Chips & Onion Dip (page 119). The chips will stick like crazy to a pan that isn't lined with parchment paper, plus it makes clean up way easier! Our favorite kind is by Kalhoof, and you can purchase it online from retailers like Amazon.

PASTRY BRUSH: A pastry brush may seem like a fancy tool, and maybe it is, but it makes things so much easier. Instead of melted garlic butter dripping off your spatula when you make Pizza Bread (page 153), you can easily and thoroughly brush it on with a pastry brush. Not to mention, pies and galettes brown best when an egg wash is applied, and a pastry brush is necessary for this. You could use a spatula in a pinch, but it would be very messy.

PIE AND TART DISHES: For sweet rolls you'll need a 9-inch pie dish, glass or ceramic. For quiche, we use a 9-inch tart pan. We like to use the kind that has a removable bottom, but you can also use a ceramic one.

POTS AND SAUCEPANS: Pots and pans are essential kitchen tools. We try to use standard sizes whenever possible. The most common sizes we use are a 2-quart saucepan and 8-quart pot. We use stainless steel here, but you can use whatever you prefer.

SLOW COOKER: A slow cooker is used as a safe method of cooking while you're not around, which is part of what we love about it! Start your slow cooker with Hearty Winter Stew (page 157) and head out for a day outside. Come back to a delicious smelling home as well as a hot dinner ready to be served. If you don't have a slow cooker, you can also use an 8-quart pot—but don't leave your house while it cooks as that can be dangerous.

SPATULAS: Having a good spatula is important for baking, especially for recipes where you need to make sure to scrape the mixing bowl entirely. For most of the recipes, any rubber spatula will do. For the Cashew Clusters (page 98), however, a high heat spatula that can go up to 500°F is required because of the butterscotch candy.

STAND MIXER: Not all of our baked recipes require a stand mixer, but it does make baking a lot easier and faster. For any of the recipes that say to mix on low with a paddle attachment, you can substitute a mixing bowl and wooden spoon—it might just take you a little bit longer. And for recipes like Whipped Cream (page 131) that call for the whisk attachment, a hand mixer with a whisk attachment will work in its place.

WAFFLE IRON: We use waffle irons for two of the recipes in the book. While we both have a square waffle iron that makes four waffles, there is no right or wrong waffle iron. Whether you have a circle iron or a square one, they will both work just fine for both recipes. The finished product may look a little different, but it will taste just as delicious!

WHISK: For recipes like waffles and pancakes, a simple whisk will get the job done.

VEGAN &
GLUTEN-FREE

We eat all kinds of foods, as long as they taste good. We believe that all food can be made delicious, even if it's vegan or gluten-free, so that's our philosophy when we're cooking and baking. We hope you will be adventurous and explore new ways of cooking and baking with vegan and gluten-free ingredients. We've included a list on page 231 of all the recipes in this book that can be made vegan or gluten-free with quick modifications, or which already happen to be vegan or gluten-free without any adjustments. For recipe modifications, you'll find notes at the end of a page indicating ingredients you can swap out, like milk or flour, to easily make the dish vegan or gluten-free.

ORGANIC CLEAN INGREDIENTS

We believe that eating organic food is like breathing clean mountain air. We hope that you will use organic ingredients for all the recipes in this book, like we do at Dessert'D Organic Bake Shop and in our home kitchens. Just like clean mountain air has less pollution, organic ingredients have less unnecessary additives, such as pesticides, chemicals, preservatives, and artificial colors. Therefore, they taste better and they really let the food shine. Bring the spirit of the mountains into your home kitchen, starting with ingredients. Here we share some of our favorites.

IN THE FRIDGE

We shop for fresh food for our fridges every week. Shopping weekly allows you to keep ingredients fresh, and most refrigerator items last for about a week.

CHEESE: We love cheese! We use a lot of it, and a lot of different kinds. When purchasing cheese, it's always better to buy blocks of cheese—even if you're going to grate it. The shredded cheeses have more additives and unnecessary ingredients in them, so we prefer to grate cheese when we need it. When cooking with cheese, another important thing for us is that the cheese has the right texture for the recipe. That said, we also believe in sometimes using what you have on hand. For example, if you don't have organic white Cheddar and you want to make our Baked Mac 'N' Cheese (page 158) it's okay to use organic yellow Cheddar instead. If you want to substitute organic feta cheese for the organic goat cheese in the Strawberry Walnut Salad (page 107), then go for it. The important thing is that your cheese is fresh, and that you use the correct amount of the cheese you're going to substitute. The best way to do that is always to measure by weight.

DAIRY: The recipes in this book call for organic whole milk. In a pinch, you could substitute 2%, but definitely not skim milk. The fat in milk provides necessary flavor for baked goods, and skim milk is closer to water than milk. One of our favorite brands of milk is

Organic Valley, but whatever the brand, you can find organic whole milk at pretty much every local market these days.

By contrast, heavy whipping cream cannot be substituted for anything else. Our favorite brand of whipping cream is Organic Valley, but many other brands out there are equally amazing. If you're going to make Whipped Cream (page 131) and know you will use it right away, then choose a heavy whipping cream that is unpasteurized. A benefit to purchasing unpasteurized milk or cream is that it retains more nutrients. If you won't use it as fast, then opt for a pasteurized version so that it doesn't go bad in your fridge after a few days.

EGGS: We use organic large eggs for all the recipes in this book. Large eggs weigh about 50 grams. If you can't find large eggs and can only get medium or extra-large, then you should beat and weigh the eggs to make sure you're getting the right amount for each recipe. You can always store the extra beaten eggs in an airtight container in the fridge and use them for egg wash on pies and galettes. In baked goods, too much or too little egg can leave your cakes or cookies too sticky or extra dry, so it's important to use the correct size. In cooking, it won't make a huge difference so there's no need to be as precise.

FATS: Butter is a main ingredient used in the recipes in this book. We use organic salted butter for all recipes. We do this because it's easier to keep one kind of butter on hand for both baking and cooking. We believe that using unsalted butter in baked goods is unnecessary. However, if you do use unsalted butter, you may want to adjust the amount of salt in the recipe to your liking.

We also use a lot of different kinds of oils such as avocado oil, coconut oil, and canola oil. For baked goods, do not substitute one kind of oil for another as they have different properties and can affect your finished desserts. However, if you're cooking something like Potato Chips & Onion Dip (page 119) and you want to use coconut oil instead of avocado oil, then we say go for it! Cooking is a little more forgiving than baking when making substitutions.

FRESH HERBS: We use a lot of fresh herbs in many of our recipes. Fresh herbs are a really easy way to bring a whole lot of flavor to a dish. So when a recipe calls for them, they are truly necessary. We don't reserve fresh herbs just for savory dishes; we also use fresh herbs in desserts like our Chocolate Sage Pecan Cake (page 221) and Raspberry Mint Galette (page 212). When purchasing fresh herbs, make sure to purchase them only a day or two ahead of when you plan to use them so that they are truly fresh. It's even better if you can purchase living herbs and keep them on your windowsill—basil, rosemary, and sage are favorites. That way, you can have them fresh all the time!

FRUITS AND VEGGIES: Using fresh fruits and veggies are always best. We know, however, that some things are not available all the time. While it's best to use fruits and veggies that are in peak season so that you get the best flavor and prices, we know that sometimes you just might crave our Glazed Blueberry Galette (page 214) out of season.

If that's the case, use frozen blueberries instead of subpar fresh ones. Just make sure to strain the fruit the night before in the fridge so that any excess water is released. Fruit is frozen at its peak, and frozen can sometimes be just as good as fresh.

IN THE PANTRY

We like to keep our pantries stocked at all times with the following basic ingredients. That way, we're ready to create a meal or dessert without much effort.

CHOCOLATE: For dark, milk, and white chocolate, the brand we use at Dessert'D is Mama Ganache. You can buy it in bulk on their website (www.mamaganache.com). Their chocolate is organic, fair trade, and it's perfect for melting, should you want to bake Double Black Diamond Brownies (page 197). For semisweet chocolate chips, we use Sunspire. These can be found at most any health food store or on Amazon.

GRAINS: Grains are ingredients that can be kept in your pantry for a few months, so it's easy to always have them on hand. We like to keep things like organic rolled oats and organic rice on hand in glass jars in the pantry.

HERBS AND SPICES: Having your pantry stocked with your favorite herbs and spices can make cooking or baking seem easier because you won't have to think about purchasing them every week. We suggest stocking up. Dried herbs and spices last for about six months in the pantry, so there's plenty

of time to use them. When we call for dried spices, like rosemary in the Rosemary Parmesan Biscotti (page 104), it's important to use dried and not fresh because the use of dry or fresh spice alters the recipe. One of our favorite brands for herbs and spices is Frontier Co-Op. This is the brand we use at Dessert'D for ingredients such as cinnamon, cloves, and black pepper. Because Frontier Co-Op is a co-op, anyone can join. You can sign up on their website (www.frontiercoop.com). You can also find this brand at most health food stores. If the recipe says just the name of the herb, such as rosemary, then it means dried. If we intend for the recipe to be made with fresh herbs, we will indicate "fresh rosemary" as the ingredient.

FLOURS: Organic all-purpose flour is the most common type of flour used in these recipes. You can purchase any kind you like; they are all fairly similar. Even your grocery store brand of organic all-purpose flour will work great.

If you would like to make some of the recipes gluten-free, the gluten-free flour we use at Dessert'D is by Namaste. It is called Organic Perfect Flour Blend, and it is what we used to test all the recipes in this book. It's made from a blend of flours—organic sweet brown rice flour, organic tapioca starch, organic brown rice flour, organic arrowroot powder, organic sorghum flour, and xanthan gum—so it really gives the gluten-free recipes the best results. If you can't find Namaste at your local health food store, it is always available on Amazon. Just do not substitute this flour for a single-ingredient flour like coconut flour as it won't give you the same results.

We also use a few specialty flours like organic coconut flour and organic almond flour. If a recipe calls for these flours specifically, it's important not to substitute them. You can find these flours at your local health food store.

NUTS AND SEEDS: When baking recipes like Roasted Rosemary Sage Almonds (page 81) or Honey Roasted Peanuts (page 82), it's important to use raw nuts because the recipe actually calls for roasting the nuts and flavoring them. When making a recipe like Sweet & Salty Trail Mix (page 85), however, the nuts should already be roasted and salted because that's where the flavor comes from. It's important to read the recipes carefully and buy the right kind of nuts. You can find organic nuts at your local market, farmers'

market, or health food store, usually in bulk. We also use flaxseeds for the Summit Bars (page 90). These can usually be bought in bulk at your health food store. They will be in the nut section.

SWEETENERS: One of our favorite sweeteners is organic cane sugar, and we use it a lot—not only at Dessert'D but also in recipes like Honey Roasted Peanuts (page 82). Organic cane sugar is darker in color than regular granulated sugar and the crystals are usually larger. Our favorite kind is by Wholesome, but most organic cane sugar is going to be very similar. Even your grocery store brand will do justice to all the recipes in this book.

Organic dark brown sugar is also used in a lot of our baked goods. Dark brown sugar has more flavor than light brown sugar, so don't swap one for the other as doing so will alter the flavor of the recipe. Wholesome makes our favorite kind of dark brown sugar as well.

Organic powdered sugar is also known as confectioners' sugar; they are the same. Wholesome makes our favorite organic powdered sugar, and it's crucial for any recipe with frosting. If you're wondering if it's really important to sift the powdered sugar when the recipe calls for it to be done—it is! Powdered sugar can clump easily after sitting in your pantry, so sifting is necessary to make smooth frosting.

Usually you think of sweeteners as ingredients for baked goods, which is appropriate. But there are other sweeteners that are used in cooking as well. We also like to put honey in our Hot Toddy (page 136) to give it more flavor. We always recommend using organic, local, raw honey as it has the most health benefits, as opposed to other types of honey.

Maple syrup is a sweetener that is crucial to waffles and pancakes. Organic maple syrup is what we use for all the recipes in this book. There are different grades of maple syrup, and your choice is a matter of personal preference. There are four grades, ranging from lightest to darkest: Fancy; Grade A Medium Amber; Grade A Dark Amber; and Grade B. The coding corresponds to color, and the darker the syrup, the stronger the flavor. We usually use Grade A or Grade B, but you can use whatever you prefer.

YEAST: We use active dry yeast for all the bread and pastry recipes in this book. The brand we like best is Giusto's, which you can find on their website (www.giustos.com). You can also buy active dry yeast at your local market. It is usually sold in small paper packets in the baking aisle. Yeast only lasts for about three or four months. If yeast has gone bad, it won't bubble at the beginning stage of the recipe. As a result, the bread or pastry won't rise. There's no point in continuing with the recipe if the yeast is not good.

Nutritional yeast is a completely different strain of yeast, and it is used as a topping or ingredient. It has an interesting flavor that really brings something extra to recipes. You can find this flaky, yellowish yeast in most bulk sections of a health food store. You'll want to pick some up to make the Strawberry Walnut Salad (page 107).

Everything Spice Mix

Makes ½ cup

I noticed that I was reaching for the same spices repeatedly while cooking. I took note of what they were and created this mix. This spice mixture really makes cooking so much easier, because it is good on so many things. Sprinkle it on Avocado Toast (page 60), toss it with veggies, or use it as a rub on meats. If you like spicy seasoning, add 1 teaspoon paprika for extra kick. — KIMMY

2 tablespoons fine sea salt

2 tablespoons black pepper

1 tablespoon garlic powder

1 tablespoon ground coriander

1 tablespoon cilantro flakes

1 tablespoon crushed
  red pepper flakes

SEA LEVEL

Follow the recipe as noted.

In a large bowl, mix all the ingredients together.

Transfer to a spice jar or an airtight container.

Store in the pantry for up to 6 months.

BREADS & PASTRIES

There's nothing I love more than eating fresh hot bread from the oven! However, it was never something that I felt like I could make. The fluffy, airy, perfect loaves always seemed too scientific and unattainable for me. I love cooking and I can throw meals together quickly based off fragrant smells and zesty flavors, but I'm not a math person and baking seemed too calculated to go with my whimsical way of throwing ingredients together.

Then I met Mimi and saw how she made baking so fun and easy! Sure, there's a science to baking things perfectly, and because Mimi is a perfectionist, every flavor and texture is flawless—a good thing when you own a delicious organic bakery. But she also showed me that experimenting is part of the journey of creating something from scratch.

When I was exploring eating vegan and gluten-free, I really started to become more fearless in my kitchen, and I became more comfortable experimenting with new ingredients and methods. When I introduced wheat back into my diet, I decided that homemade bread would be first on my list to conquer

because I wanted the ingredients to be minimal, simple, and as clean as possible. Within 24 hours of shopping for a few simple things (flour, sea salt, yeast, and a Dutch oven), to my own surprise I had two loaves of beautifully browned bread sitting in front of me. They were far from perfect, but they were homemade and delicious! All those years of thinking that bread was too hard to make—and overnight I became addicted to the scientific side of how bread rises and breathes in my mountain kitchen.

This is when my confidence with baking really bloomed. Without expectations, I began messing around with recipes for muffins and scones. With a little practice, the right ingredients, and some professional taste testing at Dessert'D, I was able to create my own pastries. My creations fueled me during my adventures in the mountains, and they gave me a skill set in the kitchen that I really needed. This chapter serves up a wide variety of delicious breads, muffins, and sweet pastries from the both of us. They are perfect for both outdoor activities and relaxing rest days.

—KIMMY

Mountain Bread

Makes 2 loaves

My mom made fresh bread frequently when I was growing up. I don't think there is anything better than the smell of a fresh loaf of bread wafting throughout the house. Once I became confident that I could bake my own bread, I dug through my recipe book for my mom's fresh-made bread that I ate all throughout my childhood. Her recipe, combined with my own journey in the kitchen, is how I created Mountain Bread. This recipe has since become my quick solution for making delicious airy bread without the worry of having a starter and a long fermentation process. It's easy to make and it's the perfect base for so many recipes like Avocado Toast (page 60) and the Crag Club Sandwich (page 150). Plus, Mimi has given my bread full approval, which is the highest honor I can think of from a master like herself. If you have only one Dutch oven, you can bake the loaves one at a time. — KIMMY

3½ cups (840 ml) warm water

1½ teaspoons active dry yeast

½ teaspoon cane sugar

4¾ cups (600 g) all-purpose flour

2 cups (340 g) whole wheat flour

1 tablespoon fine sea salt

〜〜〜 SEA LEVEL 〜〜〜

Bake at 450°F covered for 35 minutes. Remove the lids and bake for 12 to 15 minutes or until golden brown.

In the bowl of a stand mixer fitted with the dough hook, add ½ cup of the warm water, yeast, and cane sugar. Stir with a spoon to combine completely, and let sit for 5 minutes until bubbly.

Add the all-purpose flour, whole wheat flour, sea salt, and remaining 3 cups warm water in that order. Mix on low until combined into a moist and sticky dough.

Cover the bowl with plastic wrap or a warm damp dish towel. Place in a warm spot to rise. Let rise for 3 to 4 hours, or until the dough is dotted with bubbles and doubled in size.

Have two pieces of parchment paper ready and lightly flour a flat surface. Divide the dough in half and fold the edges of one of the halves up onto itself until it makes a round loaf shape. Flip the dough seam side down onto one of the pieces of parchment paper. Repeat with the other half. Place in medium bowls to hold their shape. Allow to rise 1½ to 2 hours, or until springy.

Preheat the oven to 450°F and place the Dutch ovens inside while the oven preheats.

Score the tops of each loaf and place them, with the parchment paper, into the Dutch ovens. Cover and bake for 30 minutes. Remove the lids and bake for another 12 to 15 minutes or until golden brown.

Remove from the Dutch ovens and allow to cool 15 to 30 minutes on a wire rack.

Store in an airtight container for up to 7 days.

Bagels

Makes 8 bagels

Bagels were a staple in my childhood house. They are quick, easy, and, of course, delicious. I still eat bagels all the time when I need something that's fast and will sustain me for a while. My favorite way to eat them is with simple cream cheese or butter, but you can also make Bagel French Toast (page 67) or a Bagel Sandwich (page 149). — MIMI

DOUGH

1½ cups (360 ml) hot water

2 teaspoons active dry yeast

3 tablespoons (45 g) plus
 ½ teaspoon cane sugar

3¾ cups (450 g) bread flour,
 plus extra for forming

1½ teaspoons fine sea salt

Coconut oil for greasing bowl
 and parchment paper

POACHING LIQUID

4 quarts (3.78 L) water

2 teaspoons cane sugar

½ teaspoon fine sea salt

∿∿∿ SEA LEVEL ∿∿∿

Bake at 375°F for 25 minutes or
until golden brown.

To make the dough: In the bowl of a stand mixer fitted with the dough hook, add the hot water, yeast, and ½ teaspoon cane sugar. Stir to dissolve completely. Let sit for 5 minutes until bubbly.

Add the flour, remaining 3 tablespoons cane sugar, and 1½ teaspoons sea salt to the mixing bowl and mix on low. Once the dough comes together, mix for 1 to 2 minutes on low, until smooth.

Grease a medium bowl with coconut oil. Form the dough into a ball. Place the dough in the greased bowl, cover with plastic wrap, and let rise for 1 to 2 hours or until it has doubled in size. It helps to keep it in a warm place.

Line a baking sheet with parchment paper and grease the parchment paper with coconut oil. Once the dough has doubled in size, remove from the bowl and place on a floured surface. Divide the dough evenly into eight pieces.

Form the pieces of dough into round balls, smooth the tops by pulling and tucking the dough into the bottom of the ball. They should be 3 to 4 inches in diameter. Place them on the prepared parchment paper. Cover with a kitchen towel and let rest for 30 minutes to 1 hour, until the dough feels springy.

Preheat the oven to 375°F. Then make a hole in the center of each ball of dough by pressing your finger into it. The holes should be bigger than you would think because the dough will rise and expand when baking, about 1½ inches in diameter.

To make the poaching liquid: Add the 4 quarts water to an 8-quart pot. Bring the water to a boil, then stir in the 2 teaspoons cane sugar and ½ teaspoon sea salt. When the water is boiling, drop the bagels into the water, two to three at a time, so you don't overcrowd the pot. Boil for 25 seconds on each side.

Remove the bagels from the boiling water and place back on the parchment paper. Bake for 20 minutes or until golden brown.

Store in an airtight container for up to 7 days.

CINNAMON RAISIN BAGELS

2 teaspoons cinnamon

½ cup (77 g) raisins

Add the cinnamon to the dough when you add the flour. Once the dough is done mixing, knead the raisins in by hand.

POPPY SEED BAGELS

1½ tablespoons poppy seeds

After the bagels are boiled, sprinkle the poppy seeds on top.

SPICY EVERYTHING BAGELS

2 teaspoons Everything Spice Mix (page 29)

1 teaspoon sesame seeds

1 teaspoon poppy seeds

¼ teaspoon onion powder

Mix all the ingredients together. After the bagels are boiled, sprinkle the mixture on top.

Alpine Start Muffins

Makes 12 muffins

My husband's grammy, Ginger, was a health-conscious woman who had an immaculate track record for living and eating responsibly. Whenever we visited she baked lots of muffins, so we had a morning bite that was power-packed and not too sweet. Now I make these as my grab-and-go snack for early starts on alpine adventures. Ginger always had raisins in hers, just like this recipe, but my favorite modification is to replace the raisins with ⅓ cup (57 g) fresh blueberries. — KIMMY

2½ cups (250 g) rolled oats, plus extra for topping

¼ cup (26 g) flaxseed meal

1 tablespoon baking powder

½ teaspoon fine sea salt

¼ teaspoon cinnamon

2 large eggs

1 cup (240 ml) almond milk

½ cup (176 g) maple syrup

¼ cup (50 g) mashed banana

¼ teaspoon vanilla extract

⅓ cup (51 g) raisins

············· GLUTEN-FREE ·············

Use gluten-free oats.

〜〜〜〜 SEA LEVEL 〜〜〜〜

Bake at 425°F for 15 to 18 minutes, or until a toothpick inserted in the center comes out clean.

Preheat the oven to 425°F. Line a muffin pan with liners. In a food processor, process the oats until ground into a flour. Transfer to a large mixing bowl and add the flaxseed meal, baking powder, sea salt, and cinnamon.

In a small bowl, whisk together the eggs, almond milk, maple syrup, banana, and vanilla until the texture is smooth. Add the wet ingredients into the dry ingredients and whisk until a smooth batter forms. Fold in the raisins and let the mixture sit at room temperature for 5 minutes to thicken the batter slightly.

Fill the muffin liners with ¼ cup of mixture (to about three-quarters full). Sprinkle oats on top of each muffin. Bake for 12 to 15 minutes, or until a toothpick inserted in the center comes out clean. Allow to cool completely in the muffin tin.

Store in an airtight container for up to 7 days.

Blueberry Banana Muffins

Makes 12 muffins

Banana muffins always remind me of snowboarding. My brother was obsessed with them, and this was his favorite road snack for our long drive from Kalamazoo to Harbor Springs, Michigan, every weekend. They are a sweet snack for any time of day. — MIMI

BATTER

½ cup (113 g) salted butter, softened

½ cup (113 g) packed dark brown sugar

¼ cup (57 g) cane sugar

1 teaspoon vanilla extract

2 large ripe bananas

2 large eggs

2 cups (283 g) cake flour

¾ teaspoon baking powder

½ teaspoon fine sea salt

½ teaspoon cinnamon

½ cup (120 ml) milk

1 cup (170 g) fresh blueberries

TOPPING

1 cup (127 g) all-purpose flour

½ cup (113 g) cane sugar

2 tablespoons (28 g) packed dark brown sugar

1 teaspoon cinnamon

½ cup (113 g) salted butter, melted

.... GLUTEN-FREE ....

Replace the cake flour with 1¾ cups plus 1½ tablespoons (283 g) gluten-free flour blend. And replace the all-purpose flour with ¾ cup plus 1 tablespoon (127 g) gluten-free flour blend.

〰〰 SEA LEVEL 〰〰

Follow the recipe as noted.

Preheat the oven to 350°F. Line a muffin tin with liners.

To make the batter: In the bowl of a stand mixer fitted with the paddle attachment, add the ½ cup butter, ½ cup dark brown sugar, ¼ cup cane sugar, and vanilla extract. Mix on low until combined and no chunks of butter remain. Add the bananas and eggs and mix on low until the eggs have broken up.

In a separate bowl, add the cake flour, baking powder, sea salt, and the ½ teaspoon cinnamon and whisk together. Add the milk and the flour mixture to the butter mixture and mix on low until combined. Remove the bowl from the mixer and fold in the blueberries. Fill the muffin liners all the way with batter.

To make the topping: In a medium bowl, add the all-purpose flour, ½ cup cane sugar, 2 tablespoons dark brown sugar, and 1 teaspoon cinnamon and whisk to combine. Add the ½ cup melted butter and fold with a spatula until you have a paste-like mixture. Generously crumble the mixture on top of the muffins.

Bake for 25 minutes, or until a toothpick inserted in the center comes out clean.

Store in an airtight container for up to 7 days.

Chocolate Peanut Butter Muffins

Makes 12 muffins

Sometimes a muffin is about filling you up, like Kimmy's Alpine Start Muffins
(page 37). Sometimes it's more about a dessert that can be considered breakfast, and
that's what these are. — M I M I

BATTER

½ cup (113 g) salted
  butter, softened

¾ cup (170 g) cane sugar

1 teaspoon vanilla extract

2 large ripe bananas

2 large eggs

1½ cups (212 g) cake flour

½ cup (43 g) Dutch cocoa
  powder, sifted

¾ teaspoon baking powder

½ teaspoon fine sea salt

½ cup (120 ml) heavy
  whipping cream

TOPPING

1 cup (127 g) all-purpose flour

½ cup (113 g) cane sugar

5 tablespoons (71 g) salted
  butter, melted

Scant ¼ cup (57 g) peanut butter

Heaping ¼ cup (57 g) semi-
  sweet chocolate chips

.... GLUTEN-FREE ....

Replace the cake flour with 1⅓ cups (212 g)
gluten-free flour blend. And replace the all-
purpose flour with ¾ cup plus 1 tablespoon
(127 g) gluten-free flour blend.

〜〜〜 SEA LEVEL 〜〜〜

Follow the recipe as noted.

Preheat the oven to 350°F. Line a muffin tin with liners.

To make the batter: In the bowl of a stand mixer fitted with the
paddle attachment, add the ½ cup butter, ¾ cup cane sugar, and
vanilla extract. Mix on low until combined and no chunks of
butter remain. Add the bananas and eggs and mix on low until the
eggs have broken up.

In a separate bowl, add the cake flour, cocoa powder, baking
powder, and sea salt and whisk together. Add the cream and
the flour mixture to the butter mixture and mix on low until
combined. Fill muffin liners all the way with batter.

To make the topping: In a medium bowl, add the all-purpose flour
and ½ cup cane sugar and whisk to combine.

In a separate bowl, add the melted butter and peanut butter and
mix together. Add to the flour mixture and fold with a spatula
until you have a paste-like mixture. Add in the chocolate chips
and generously crumble the mixture on top of the muffins.

Bake for 25 minutes, or until a toothpick inserted in center comes
out clean.

Store in an airtight container for up to 7 days.

Raspberry Almond Scones

Makes 8 scones

This breakfast treat isn't your typical scone. Instead, it's denser and packed with more nutrients. It's the perfect snack to fuel your adventures or to leave on the counter for people on the go. Since I spend most of my time running around the mountains, I'm always looking for snacks that are packed with protein and deliciousness, and that leave me feeling full for longer. These do just that! **— KIMMY**

SCONES

2¾ cups (272 g) almond flour, plus extra for dusting

Scant ⅓ cup (107 g) maple syrup

¼ cup (60 ml) unsweetened almond milk

1 tablespoon (15 ml) fresh lemon juice

1 teaspoon vanilla extract

½ cup (49 g) coconut flour

¼ cup (57 g) cane sugar

1 tablespoon baking powder

½ teaspoon fine sea salt

½ teaspoon lemon zest

¼ cup plus 1 tablespoon (71 g) coconut oil

1 cup (142 g) raspberries, halved

½ cup (67 g) blanched slivered almonds, plus extra for topping

GLAZE

1 cup (142 g) powdered sugar, sifted

1½ to 2 tablespoons (22 to 30 ml) water

〰〰 SEA LEVEL 〰〰

Follow the recipe as noted.

To make the scones: Line a baking sheet with parchment paper, and sprinkle with almond flour (to prevent burning).

In a small bowl, whisk together the maple syrup, almond milk, lemon juice, and vanilla. Allow to sit while you mix dry ingredients.

In the bowl of a stand mixer fitted with the paddle attachment, add the almond flour, coconut flour, cane sugar, baking powder, sea salt, and lemon zest and mix on low for four to five rotations to combine completely. Add the coconut oil to the dry ingredients by pinching it into solid clumps over the bowl. Mix on low until it looks like wet sand.

Slowly add in the liquid mixture to the dry ingredients and mix on low until a dough forms. Remove the mixing bowl from the mixer and carefully fold in the raspberries and almonds.

Transfer the dough to the prepared baking sheet and form into an 8-inch disk. Cut the disk into eight triangles, like a pizza. Space each piece ½ inch apart. Place in the fridge for 15 minutes. Preheat the oven to 400°F.

Remove from the fridge and bake for 25 to 30 minutes, or until golden brown. Let cool completely on the baking sheet.

To make the glaze: In a small mixing bowl, whisk together the powdered sugar and water until smooth. Drizzle the scones with the glaze and top with more almonds.

Store in an airtight container for up to 5 days.

Chocolate Sweet Rolls

Makes 8 rolls

Rich, decadent, and not too sweet: I use Dutch cocoa powder instead of a sweeter
chocolate to make these rolls. This allows the glaze to be just sweet enough. — MIMI

DOUGH

¼ cup (60 ml) hot water

2 teaspoons active dry yeast

¼ cup (57 g) plus ½ teaspoon
  cane sugar

¼ cup (57 g) salted butter

¾ cup (180 ml) milk

3½ cups (446 g) all-purpose flour

1 teaspoon fine sea salt

1 large egg

FILLING

⅓ cup (28 g) Dutch cocoa
  powder, sifted

¼ cup (57 g) cane sugar

½ cup (113 g) salted
  butter, softened

GLAZE

1 cup (142 g) powdered sugar, sifted

3 tablespoons (45 ml) milk

〜〜〜 SEA LEVEL 〜〜〜
Bake at 350°F for 40 minutes, or until
golden brown.

To make the dough: In the bowl of a stand mixer fitted with the
dough hook, add the hot water, yeast, and ½ teaspoon cane sugar.
Stir to combine and let sit for 5 minutes until bubbly.

In a small saucepan over medium heat, add the ¼ cup butter and
¾ cup milk. Stir until completely melted. Remove from the heat.

Add the flour, ¼ cup cane sugar, and sea salt to the mixing bowl
in that order. Add the egg and the milk mixture and knead on low
for 3 to 5 minutes, until a smooth dough forms. Place the dough in
a greased bowl. Cover the bowl with plastic wrap and let rise for
1 to 3 hours, until doubled in size.

Preheat the oven to 350°F and grease a baking dish, either a
9-inch circle dish or an 11-by-7-inch dish.

To make the filling: In a small bowl, combine the cocoa and
¼ cup cane sugar. Set aside.

On a floured surface, roll out the dough to a rectangle that is about
12-by-16 inches. Using a spatula, spread the ½ cup butter all over
the rolled-out dough. Sprinkle the sugar and cocoa mixture on top
of the butter. Starting at the longer side, fold the dough over and
start to roll the dough until it is completely rolled into a log. Trim
off the edges and cut the dough log into eight rolls.

Place the rolls in the prepared baking dish and bake for
35 minutes, or until golden brown. Allow to cool for 5 to
10 minutes.

To make the glaze: In a mixing bowl, add the powdered sugar and
3 tablespoons milk and whisk until you have a smooth glaze. Pour
the glaze over the top of the warm sweet rolls.

Store in the fridge for up to 3 days.

Almond Elderberry Sweet Rolls

Makes 8 rolls

On cold fall days, I love waking up to the smell of cinnamon rolls baking. The beginning of the ski season always brought on lazy mornings because there was no rush to get up to the mountain, so this gave me time to enjoy them. Elderberries grow wild in the Eastern Sierra, so I've created a new twist on cinnamon rolls to incorporate these sweet berries. — MIMI

DOUGH

¼ cup (60 ml) hot water

2 teaspoons active dry yeast

¼ cup (57 g) plus ½ teaspoon cane sugar

¼ cup (57 g) salted butter

¾ cup (180 ml) milk

3½ cups (446 g) all-purpose flour

1 teaspoon fine sea salt

1 large egg

FILLING

¼ cup (57 g) salted butter, softened

1 tablespoon almond butter

½ cup (113 g) cane sugar

1 teaspoon cinnamon

GLAZE

1 cup (142 g) powdered sugar, sifted

3 tablespoons (45 ml) milk

1 tablespoon elderberry preserves

〰〰〰 SEA LEVEL 〰〰〰

Bake at 350°F for 40 minutes, or until golden brown.

To make the dough: In the bowl of a stand mixer fitted with the dough hook, add the hot water, yeast, and ½ teaspoon cane sugar. Stir to combine and let sit for 5 minutes until bubbly.

In a small saucepan over medium heat, add the ¼ cup butter and ¾ cup milk. Stir until completely melted. Remove from the heat.

Add the flour, ¼ cup cane sugar, and sea salt to the mixing bowl in that order. Add the egg and the milk mixture and knead on low for 3 to 5 minutes until the dough is smooth. Place the dough in a greased bowl. Cover the bowl with plastic wrap and let rise for 1 to 3 hours, until doubled in size.

Preheat the oven to 350°F and grease a baking dish, either a 9-inch circle dish or an 11-by-7-inch dish.

To make the filling: In a small bowl, add the ¼ cup butter and almond butter and stir to combine completely.

In medium bowl, combine the ½ cup cane sugar and cinnamon.

On a floured surface, roll out the dough to a rectangle that is about 12-by-16 inches. Using a spatula, spread the butter mixture all over the rolled-out dough. Sprinkle the sugar and cinnamon mixture to completely cover the butter. Starting at the longer side, fold the dough over and start to roll the dough until it is completely rolled into a log. Trim off the edges and cut the dough log into eight pieces.

Place in your prepared baking dish and bake for 35 minutes, or until golden brown. Allow to cool for 5 to 10 minutes.

To make the glaze: In a mixing bowl, add the powdered sugar, 3 tablespoons milk, and elderberry preserves, and whisk until you have a smooth glaze. Pour the glaze over the top of the warm sweet rolls.

Store in the fridge for up to 3 days.

Maple Brown Sugar Snack Tarts

Makes 6 snack tarts

Many toaster pastry recipes out there tell you to make a pie dough. However, traditional Pop-Tarts are not made with pie dough, and this recipe's dough is somewhere between a pie and cookie dough. It makes for the most authentic homemade Pop-Tarts I have ever tasted. —MIMI

DOUGH

¼ cup (57 grams) salted butter, softened

¼ cup (57 g) cane sugar

¼ cup (35 g) powdered sugar, sifted

⅛ teaspoon cinnamon

2 cups (255 g) all-purpose flour, plus extra for rolling

1 large egg yolk

¼ cup water

FILLING

½ cup (113 g) packed dark brown sugar

¼ cup (32 g) all-purpose flour

¼ cup (60 ml) heavy whipping cream

1 teaspoon cinnamon

GLAZE

¾ cup (106 g) powdered sugar, sifted

1 tablespoon (15 ml) milk

1 tablespoon (22 g) maple syrup

〰〰〰 SEA LEVEL 〰〰〰

Bake at 350°F for 30 minutes, or until golden brown.

Preheat the oven to 350°F. Line a baking sheet with parchment paper and have a small dish with water ready.

To make the dough: In the bowl of a stand mixer fitted with the paddle attachment, add the butter, cane sugar, ¼ cup powdered sugar, and ⅛ teaspoon cinnamon. Mix on low until combined and no chunks of butter remain. Add the 2 cups flour, egg yolk, and ¼ cup water and mix on low until combined into a stiff dough.

To make the filling: In a medium bowl, add the brown sugar, ¼ cup flour, heavy whipping cream, and 1 teaspoon cinnamon. Mix together until a paste-like mixture forms and set aside.

On a floured surface, knead the dough with extra flour until it is a smooth consistency. Roll out the dough into an 18-by-9-inch rectangle that is ⅛-inch thick. Trim off the edges, cut in half longways, then cut into six pieces on each side, so you have 12 rectangles that are about 3-by-4 inches.

Place half the rectangles on the parchment paper and spoon about 1 tablespoon of filling onto each one. Then mold and flatten the filling to be a rectangle, leaving a small space around the border. Dip your finger in the prepared dish of water and trace the border of each rectangle. Then place the matching rectangles on top, pressing down to seal them. Using a fork, push down on all sides to crimp the tarts closed. Using a butter knife, slit the tarts to create three vents on each one.

Bake for 25 minutes, or until golden brown. Let cool completely on the baking sheet.

To make the glaze: In a medium bowl, add the ¾ cup powdered sugar, milk, and maple syrup and whisk until combined into a smooth glaze. Using a butter knife, frost each tart.

Store in an airtight container for up to 5 days.

Cherry Snack Tarts

Makes 6 snack tarts

Cherry Pop-Tarts were something I lived for as a child, though I rarely got to enjoy them because they weren't one of our approved breakfast options. If my mom had this recipe, maybe they would have been. — MIMI

FILLING

20 fresh cherries,
  destemmed and pitted

½ cup (113 g) cane sugar

¼ cup water

DOUGH

¼ cup (57 g) salted butter, softened

¼ cup (57 g) cane sugar

¼ cup (35 g) powdered sugar, sifted

2 cups (255 g) all-purpose
  flour, plus extra for rolling

1 large egg yolk

¼ cup water

GLAZE

1¼ cups (185 g) powdered
  sugar, sifted

2½ tablespoons (37 ml) milk

India Tree Nature's Colors
  Red Decorating Sugar

〰〰〰 SEA LEVEL 〰〰〰

Bake at 350°F for 30 minutes, or until
golden brown.

To make the filling: In a small saucepan, add the cherries, ½ cup cane sugar, and ¼ cup water. Put over high heat and allow the sugar to dissolve. Start to mash the cherries with a spatula and let them burst. Allow the mixture to boil for 1 to 2 minutes. Lower the heat to medium and simmer until the mixture has reduced by half and is a thick consistency, 10 to 15 minutes. Place in the fridge and allow to chill overnight.

Preheat the oven to 350°F. Line a baking sheet with parchment paper and have a small dish with water ready.

To make the dough: In the bowl of a stand mixer fitted with the paddle attachment, add the butter, ¼ cup cane sugar, and ¼ cup powdered sugar. Mix on low until combined and no chunks of butter remain. Add the flour, egg yolk, and ¼ cup water and mix on low until combined.

On a floured surface, knead the dough with extra flour until it is a smooth consistency. Roll out the dough into an 18-by-9-inch rectangle that is ⅛-inch thick. Trim off the edges, cut in half longways, then cut into 6 pieces on each side, so you have 12 rectangles that are about 3-by-4 inches.

Place half the rectangles on the parchment paper and spoon about 1 tablespoon of filling onto each one. Dip your finger in the prepared dish of water and trace the border of each rectangle. Then place the matching rectangles on top, pressing down to seal them. Using a fork, push down on all sides to crimp the tarts closed. Using a butter knife, slit the tarts to create three vents on each one.

Bake for 25 minutes, or until golden brown. Let cool completely on the baking sheet.

To make the glaze: In a medium bowl, add the 1¼ cups powdered sugar and milk and whisk until combined into a smooth glaze. Using a butter knife, frost each tart and sprinkle with red sugar.

Store in an airtight container for up to 5 days.

EATS

Breakfast is your first opportunity of the day to eat, which is why we call this chapter Eats. Many of these recipes can be enjoyed for days at a time, like bagels, waffles, and granola. So take the time to bake them, and then savor them all week long. While these recipes are inspired by breakfast, they can also be made for any time of day: They make hearty snacks, the perfect brunch spread, or even a quick dinner.

I wasn't a morning person until I started snowboarding. You kinda have to be in order to have the most fun; otherwise you miss out on all the fresh snow. As a teenager I went from sleeping until 10 a.m. to getting up before the sun. Breakfast used to be something I ate leisurely while lounging around on the weekends. But once snowboarding took over, breakfast turned into fuel for my morning on the mountain, and it became my favorite meal of the day. Ham & Cheese Omelets (page 72) became part of my weekend routine, and I've been eating eggs for breakfast (in different varieties) ever since.

My mornings are a little different now than they used to be, but they're similar in that I still need to start my day with some good eats. For years, breakfast was the only meal my husband and I were able to enjoy together, because working long hours at the bake shop gave me limited time for meals at home. This is another reason why it's my favorite meal, and one of the primary reasons I decided to open my bake shop at 11 a.m. each day, and only serve desserts. It's really important to me to be able to spend mornings how I want. Whether my adventure is in the kitchen or outside in the mountains, I feel so much better when I am fueled with breakfast. —MIMI

First Chair Granola

Makes 9 cups

This granola combines all my favorite things: oats, pecans, maple syrup, and, of course, coffee. I pour myself a bowl of this granola with almond milk when I'm craving something crunchy and full of flavor. I also love bringing a little stash in my pocket for a day outside. —KIMMY

½ cup (113 g) coconut oil

¼ cup (57 g) packed
dark brown sugar

3 cups (298 g) rolled oats

½ cup (57 g) sliced almonds
with their skins

½ cup (64 g) pecan halves

½ cup (32 g) unsweetened
wide flake coconut

2 tablespoons ground coffee

¼ teaspoon ground vanilla bean

¼ teaspoon cinnamon

½ cup (176 g) maple syrup

1 cup (142 g) chopped
dark chocolate

·············· GLUTEN-FREE ··············

Use gluten-free oats.

〜〜〜 SEA LEVEL 〜〜〜

Bake at 325°F for 25 minutes, remove
from the oven, and stir to rotate the
granola. Bake again for 25 minutes or
until the granola seems dry.

Preheat the oven to 325°F. Line a baking sheet with parchment paper.

In a small saucepan, add the coconut oil and brown sugar. Cook over medium heat until melted and then remove from the heat.

In a large bowl, combine the oats, almonds, pecans, coconut, ground coffee, vanilla bean, and cinnamon. Mix to combine completely. Pour the maple syrup and the coconut oil mixture over the oats mixture and stir until completely coated.

Spread the granola across the baking sheet evenly. Bake for 20 minutes, remove from the oven, and stir to rotate the granola. Bake again for 20 minutes, or until the granola seems dry. Remove the granola from the oven and let cool completely on the baking sheet.

Once cool, add the granola and dark chocolate to a mixing bowl and combine completely.

Store in an airtight container for up to 1 month.

Honey Raisin Granola

Makes 9 cups

When I lived in Vermont at boarding school, my daily routine started with raisin granola because I could grab it in less than a minute, which meant more sleep. My favorite way to eat it is in a bowl with milk, just like I used to do on my way to the mountain. — MIMI

3 cups (298 g) rolled oats

¾ cup (85 g) walnuts

2 cups (128 g) wide flake unsweetened coconut

½ cup plus 2 tablespoons (142 g) cane sugar

½ cup (113 g) coconut oil

½ cup water

3 tablespoons (64 g) raw honey

1 tablespoon plus 2 teaspoons (28 g) light corn syrup

1 teaspoon vanilla extract

½ teaspoon fine sea salt

¾ cup (113 g) raisins

············ GLUTEN-FREE ············

Use gluten-free oats.

〰〰〰 SEA LEVEL 〰〰〰

Bake at 325°F for 25 minutes, remove from the oven, and stir to rotate the granola. Bake again for 25 minutes, or until golden brown.

Preheat the oven to 325°F. Line a baking sheet with parchment paper.

In a large mixing bowl, add the oats, walnuts, and half the coconut. Set aside.

In a small saucepan, add the cane sugar, coconut oil, water, honey, and corn syrup. Cook on medium heat until everything is combined. Remove from the heat and add in the vanilla extract and sea salt. Stir to combine completely. Pour the sugar mixture over the oat mixture and fold to combine and completely coat the oats.

Transfer to the prepared baking sheet and spread out as evenly as possible. Bake for 20 minutes, remove from the oven, and stir to rotate the granola. Bake again for 20 minutes, or until golden brown. Let cool completely on the baking sheet.

Once cool, add the granola, remaining coconut flakes, and raisins to a large mixing bowl. Mix to combine completely.

Store in an airtight container for up to 1 month.

Baked Breakfast Cups

Makes 12 breakfast cups

As a professional snowboarder and an adventure enthusiast, I leave the house before the sun is up most mornings. I designed these baked breakfast cups for breakfast on the go. I make them ahead of time, put half of them in the refrigerator, and throw the rest of them in the freezer. What I love most about these is how easy they are to make and that you can put a variety of ingredients that you like inside. — KIMMY

2 cups (113 g) broccoli florets, destemmed

10 large eggs

¾ cup (68 g) grated white Cheddar cheese

¼ cup (11 g) chopped fresh chives

1½ teaspoons garlic powder

½ teaspoon fine sea salt

Canola oil cooking spray

〰〰〰 SEA LEVEL 〰〰〰

Bake at 400°F for 20 to 24 minutes, until the tops are slightly golden brown.

Preheat the oven to 400°F. Line a muffin pan with liners.

Steam the broccoli by adding about an inch of water into a small saucepan. Place a steamer basket in the saucepan, add the broccoli, and cover with a lid. Let steam for about 5 minutes or until the broccoli is tender and bright in color. Remove from the heat and chop into ½-inch pieces.

In a large bowl, whisk the eggs together. Add ½ cup of the cheese, chives, garlic powder, and sea salt to the eggs and whisk to combine. Add the chopped broccoli to the egg mixture and stir thoroughly.

Grease the muffin liners with canola oil cooking spray to prevent sticking. Using a ⅓ measuring cup, scoop the egg mixture into the muffin tins to approximately two-thirds full.

Sprinkle the remaining ¼ cup cheese evenly on top of each egg cup. Bake for 16 to 20 minutes, until the tops are slightly golden brown.

Store in the fridge for up to 3 days.

Avocado Toast

Makes 4 slices

If I had to choose one type of food to eat for the rest of my life, it would be avocado toast. The combination of fresh-made bread, creamy avocado, and delicious seasoning is my idea of a perfect breakfast. I eat this almost daily. It wasn't until I started making my own bread, however, that I really fell in love with this simple but satisfying staple. To make it more filling, I sometimes top it with hemp seeds, nutritional yeast, and a fried egg. —KIMMY

4 slices Mountain Bread (page 33)

2 medium avocados

1 teaspoon Everything Spice Mix (page 29)

〜〜〜 SEA LEVEL 〜〜〜

Follow the recipe as noted.

Toast 4 slices Mountain Bread. While toasting, half and pit the avocados.

Once the bread is toasted to your liking, spread half an avocado onto each slice. Sprinkle each slice with Everything Spice Mix.

Honey Graham Pancakes

Makes 12 pancakes

Pancakes will always remind me of weekends at our ski cabin. There's nothing like having a hot breakfast on a crisp, cold morning. In this recipe I have taken maple syrup to the next level by adding honey butter. — MIMI

BATTER

2 whole (52 g) graham crackers

½ cup (113 g) salted butter

1½ cups (191 g) all-purpose flour

¼ cup plus 2 tablespoons (85 g) cane sugar

1 tablespoon baking powder

¼ teaspoon fine sea salt

2 large eggs

1 cup (240 ml) milk

¼ cup (59 g) heavy whipping cream

1 teaspoon vanilla extract

Canola oil cooking spray

SYRUP

1 tablespoon (14 g) salted butter

1 tablespoon (21 g) raw honey

½ cup (176 g) maple syrup

Blackberries for serving

·············· **GLUTEN-FREE** ··············

Use gluten-free graham crackers; make sure to weigh them (52 g) because gluten-free grahams are not always the same size. Replace the all-purpose flour with scant a 1¼ cups (191 g) gluten-free flour blend.

〰〰〰 **SEA LEVEL** 〰〰〰

Follow the recipe as noted.

To make the batter: In a food processor, process the graham crackers until fine. Set aside.

In a small saucepan over medium heat, melt the ½ cup butter. Let cool to room temperature before next step.

In a medium mixing bowl, add the graham crackers, flour, cane sugar, baking powder, and sea salt and whisk together.

In the saucepan with the butter, add the eggs, milk, whipping cream, and vanilla extract and whisk together. Then slowly pour the liquid mixture into the dry ingredients in the mixing bowl while whisking until you have a smooth batter.

In a medium frying pan over medium heat, grease the pan well with the cooking spray. Pour the pancake batter into the frying pan, about a ¼ cup for each pancake. Wait for the top of the pancake to start bubbling, for 1½ to 2 minutes. Flip the pancake and cook until done, for 1½ to 2 minutes on the second side as well. Repeat until the batter is gone.

To make the syrup: In a small saucepan, melt the 1 tablespoon butter and honey. Remove from the heat. Add the maple syrup and whisk together until smooth.

Pumpkin Spice Pancakes

Makes 15 pancakes

These fall-inspired pancakes are perfect to make when you have extra pumpkin lying around. You can even make the batter the night before and stick it in the fridge. Just let the batter come to room temperature the next morning before frying up the pancakes. — MIMI

½ cup (113 g) salted butter

1¼ cups (177 g) whole wheat pastry flour

¼ cup (57 g) cane sugar

1 teaspoon cinnamon

½ teaspoon cloves

½ teaspoon ginger

Pinch of nutmeg

1 tablespoon baking powder

¼ teaspoon fine sea salt

1 large egg

1 cup (240 ml) milk

½ cup (123 g) pumpkin puree

1 teaspoon vanilla extract

Canola oil cooking spray for greasing the pan

Maple syrup, butter, and sliced apples for serving

.... GLUTEN-FREE ....

Replace the pastry flour with 1 cup plus 2 tablespoons (177 g) gluten-free flour blend.

~~~~~ SEA LEVEL ~~~~~

Follow the recipe as noted.

In a small saucepan over medium heat, melt the butter. Let cool to room temperature before the next step.

In a medium mixing bowl, add the pastry flour, cane sugar, cinnamon, cloves, ginger, nutmeg, baking powder, and sea salt and whisk together.

In the saucepan with the butter, add the egg, milk, pumpkin, and vanilla extract and whisk together. Then slowly add into the dry ingredients while whisking until you have a smooth batter.

In a medium frying pan over medium heat, grease the pan well with the cooking spray.

Pour the pancake batter into the frying pan, about a scant ¼ cup for each pancake. Wait for the top of the pancake to start bubbling, for 1½ to 2 minutes. Flip the pancake and cook until done, for 1½ to 2 minutes on the second side as well. Repeat until the batter is gone.

Serve with maple syrup, butter, and sliced apples.

Bagel French Toast

Makes 6 pieces

French toast has always been my favorite breakfast indulgence. I love eating French toast made with cinnamon raisin bread, so I thought, *Why not make it on a cinnamon raisin bagel?* The bagel makes an amazing vessel for butter, eggs, and spices because it's thick and can soak up liquid well without breaking. When I have extra time in the morning, this is my favorite breakfast to make. —MIMI

3 Cinnamon Raisin Bagels (page 35)

2 large eggs

2 tablespoons (30 ml) heavy whipping cream

1 teaspoon cinnamon

Pinch of cloves

3 tablespoons (42 g) salted butter

Powdered sugar for dusting

Maple syrup for serving

~~~~ SEA LEVEL ~~~~

Follow the recipe as noted.

Slice the bagels in half. In a shallow bowl or dish, add the eggs, cream, cinnamon, and cloves. Whisk together until combined.

In a medium frying pan, add 1 tablespoon of the butter and turn to medium heat. Allow the butter to melt and coat the pan.

Soak two halves of a bagel in the egg mixture and add the halves to the pan. Cook both sides until golden brown, about 1 to 2 minutes per side. Repeat with the remaining bagel slices, adding 1 tablespoon butter to the pan each time.

Dust with powdered sugar and serve with maple syrup.

Chocolate Waffles

Makes 10 waffles

Waffles were something we saved for special occasions. They require a little extra time and effort, but when you do have the time, they are completely worth it. You can make this waffle batter the night before, stick it in the fridge, and remove it in the morning. This will help you get out of the house faster and into the mountains with a belly full of waffles. — MIMI

BATTER

½ cup (71 g) finely chopped milk chocolate

1¼ cups (283 g) salted butter

1½ cups (360 ml) milk

1¾ cups plus 2 tablespoons (240 g) all-purpose flour

½ cup (43 g) Dutch cocoa powder, sifted

¼ cup (57 g) cane sugar

1 teaspoon fine sea salt

1 teaspoon baking powder

½ teaspoon ground vanilla bean

4 large eggs

TOPPING

Whipped Cream (page 131)

6 ounces (170 g) strawberries, chopped in quarters

.... GLUTEN-FREE ....

Replace the all-purpose flour with 1½ cups (234 g) gluten-free flour blend.

〜〜〜 SEA LEVEL 〜〜〜

Follow the recipe as noted.

To create a double boiler, fill a small saucepan with water and place a heatproof bowl on top; do not let the bowl touch the water. Place over high and melt the milk chocolate in the bowl. Remove from the heat and set aside.

Add the butter and milk to a medium saucepan; put over medium heat. Stir consistently until the butter has melted. Remove from the heat.

In a medium mixing bowl, add the flour, cocoa powder, cane sugar, sea salt, baking powder, and vanilla bean and whisk together. Add the melted chocolate, eggs, and the milk mixture to the flour mixture and whisk together until smooth.

Turn on a waffle iron and allow to preheat. Measure out ½ cup per waffle (I use a square iron for this recipe). Allow to cook for 2½ minutes (or follow instructions on your waffle iron). Remove the waffle from the waffle iron and repeat until the batter is gone.

Serve with the Whipped Cream and strawberries.

Protein Waffles

Makes 4 waffles

My mom would make waffles only on rare weekends that we didn't have plans. They were a symbol of a relaxing day together. The sugary, sweet smell of them cooking still makes my mouth water. As I began playing with ingredients, I learned how to make my favorite morning recipes less sweet and more protein-packed for big days outdoors. With that purpose in mind, I created this delicious and adventure-driven recipe. It fuels the biggest days but is also perfect for a casual Sunday morning brunch. — KIMMY

¼ cup (25 g) rolled oats

⅓ cup (63 g) chia seeds

¼ cup (26 g) flaxseed meal

2 teaspoons baking powder

¼ teaspoon fine sea salt

¼ teaspoon cinnamon

4 large eggs

2 large egg whites

½ cup (120 ml) almond milk

¼ cup (57 g) unsweetened applesauce

1 tablespoon (14 g) coconut oil, melted, plus extra for greasing

¼ teaspoon vanilla extract

Bananas, blueberries, and maple syrup for serving

In a food processor, process the oats until you have a flour. Transfer to a medium bowl. Add the chia seeds, flaxseed meal, baking powder, sea salt, and cinnamon to the bowl with the oat flour and whisk together.

In a large bowl, mix together the eggs, egg whites, almond milk, applesauce, coconut oil, and vanilla extract. Add the dry ingredients to the wet ingredients and whisk until you have a smooth batter. Use a spatula to scrape the sides of the bowl.

Allow the batter to sit at room temperature for 25 to 30 minutes so the flaxseed, oats, and chia seeds can thicken the batter. Stir occasionally.

Turn on the waffle iron and allow to preheat. Lightly grease the waffle iron with coconut oil. Measure out ½ cup per waffle (I use a square iron for this recipe and pour the batter into the middle). Close the lid and cook each waffle for 3 minutes (or follow instructions on your waffle iron).

Serve with bananas, blueberries, and maple syrup.

········· GLUTEN-FREE ·········

Use gluten-free oats.

〰〰〰 SEA LEVEL 〰〰〰

Follow the recipe as noted.

Ham & Cheese Omelet

Makes 1 omelet

One of the menu items at Dad's Diner was ham and cheese omelets. My dad would fry these babies up so fast and so perfectly every single time, I'm still jealous at the memory. Patience is not my virtue and I always have a difficult time making omelets, so in a worst case scenario I turn this into a scramble. Why not, it tastes just as good! —MIMI

2 large eggs

Canola oil cooking spray

¼ cup (14 g) shredded sharp Cheddar cheese

1 slice honey ham, chopped

Fine sea salt

Black pepper

〜〜〜 **SEA LEVEL** 〜〜〜

Follow the recipe as noted.

In a medium bowl, whisk together the eggs. Generously grease a small frying pan with the cooking spray. (Using butter here won't give the best results as omelets take time, and the butter can brown, so that's why it's best to use canola oil spray. Another high-heat oil such as avocado or coconut would also work.)

Heat the pan over low heat and pour the eggs in. Add the cheese and ham on one side of the egg. Let it sit until you can visibly see the omelet cooking around the edges, for 1 to 4 minutes. Once the omelet is partially cooked, fold over the side without the ham and cheese. Continue to cook until it seems dry, flip when able to, and continue to cook to your liking.

Salt and pepper to taste.

Spinach & Bacon Quiche

Makes one 9-inch quiche

Growing up I thought quiche was reserved for once a year at Mother's Day brunch. This, however, is not your mother's quiche. Instead, it's a fun twist on bacon and eggs. Baking these two breakfast favorites inside a quiche crust just makes it a little more fun to eat. — MIMI

CRUST

¾ cup (95 g) all-purpose flour

½ teaspoon cane sugar

6 tablespoons (85 g)
  salted butter, cold

3 tablespoons (45 ml) cold water

FILLING

4 large eggs

½ cup (120 ml) milk

⅓ cup (30 g) grated sharp
  Cheddar cheese

⅓ cup (14 g) spinach

½ cup (56 g) thinly
  sliced cauliflower

2 slices applewood smoked
  bacon, cooked and chopped

1 tablespoon finely chopped chives

〜〜〜〜 SEA LEVEL 〜〜〜〜

Bake at 350°F for 25 minutes for the first parbake, remove the beans and parchment paper, and bake again for 15 minutes. Once filled, bake for 40 minutes, until set.

To make the crust: In the bowl of a stand mixer fitted with the paddle attachment, add the flour and cane sugar.

Remove the butter from the fridge and cut the stick into four pieces. From there, chop the pieces into small cubes; the smaller the cubes, the flakier the crust. Add the cold cubed butter to the flour mixture.

Measure out the cold water and have ready. Turn the mixer on low and slowly start to incorporate the flour, cane sugar, and butter. Gradually turn the mixer to medium speed. Once the butter mixture looks like wet sand, immediately add in all the water. As soon as the dough comes together, stop the mixer.

Using your hands, form the dough into a disk and place it in plastic wrap. Chill in the fridge for at least 6 hours or overnight.

Preheat the oven to 350°F. On a floured surface, roll out the crust to ¼-inch thick. Place in a quiche pan and form against the sides. Fold over any edges to create even sides that are flush with the edge of the pan.

Place a piece of parchment paper into the quiche pan and fill with beans or pie weights. Parbake the crust for 20 minutes, remove the beans and parchment paper, and bake again for 10 minutes.

To make the filling: In a medium bowl, whisk together the eggs and milk. Add in the cheese, spinach, cauliflower, bacon, and chives and mix together. Transfer to the quiche crust and spread evenly.

Bake for 35 minutes, until set.

Store in the fridge for up to 5 days.

Veggie Quiche

Makes one 9-inch quiche

Quiche is one of my favorite meals for any time of day, be it breakfast, lunch, or dinner!
In order to keep it interesting, I love coming up with new flavors. Purple potatoes have
more antioxidants than regular potatoes, and they give this quiche so much color.
Adding an herb to the crust really makes this quiche stand out even more. — MIMI

CRUST

¾ cup (95 g) all-purpose flour

½ teaspoon cane sugar

½ teaspoon oregano

6 tablespoons (85 g)
    salted butter, cold

3 tablespoons (45 ml) cold water

FILLING

4 large eggs

½ cup (120 ml) milk

⅓ cup (30 g) grated white
    Cheddar cheese

⅓ cup (14 g) spinach

2 medium mushrooms, thinly sliced

1 small purple potato, thinly sliced

1 clove garlic, minced

SEA LEVEL

Bake at 350°F for 25 minutes for the
first parbake, remove the beans and
parchment paper, and bake again
for 15 minutes. Once filled, bake for
40 minutes, until set.

To make the crust: In the bowl of a stand mixer fitted with the
paddle attachment, add the flour, cane sugar, and oregano. Turn
on low for two to three rotations to combine the dry ingredients.

Remove the butter from the fridge and cut the stick into four
pieces. From there, chop the pieces into small cubes; the smaller
the cubes, the flakier the crust. Add the cold cubed butter to the
flour mixture.

Measure out the cold water and have ready. Turn the mixer on low
and slowly start to incorporate all the flour, cane sugar, oregano,
and butter. Gradually turn the mixer to medium speed. Once the
butter mixture looks like wet sand, immediately add in all the
water. As soon as the dough comes together, stop the mixer.

Form the dough into a disk and wrap in plastic wrap. Allow to cool
in the fridge for at least 6 hours or overnight.

Preheat the oven to 350°F. On a floured surface, roll out the crust
to ¼-inch thick. Place in a 9-inch quiche pan and form against the
sides. Fold over any edges to create even sides that are flush with
the edge of the pan.

Place a piece of parchment paper into the quiche pan and fill with
beans or pie weights. Parbake the crust for 20 minutes, remove
the beans and parchment paper, and bake again for 10 minutes.

To make the filling: In a medium bowl, whisk together the eggs
and milk. Add in the cheese, spinach, mushrooms, potato, and
garlic and mix together.

Transfer to the quiche crust and spread evenly. Bake for
35 minutes, until set.

Store in the fridge for up to 5 days.

MADE for ADVENTURE

O*ur bodies are designed to move,* and mine in particular is made for adventure. Ever since I was little I have been an early riser, and I love spending time outside no matter the time of year. Growing up in the mountains, it was easy to be a fearless child and I always found ways to test my boundaries with adventure-filled days. Whether it was playing in streams, making forts in the woods, or making snow angels in the powder, I always came home exhausted and hungry, but smiling and satisfied.

As an adult and a professional athlete, not much has changed. I still have a desire to explore my limits and push past my comfort zone from dawn until dusk. There have been many long days riding on the mountain when I've thought about going in or stopping for lunch, but I never ended up doing it because taking a break didn't sound appealing. I can't tell you how many times I have gone out for a short hike and it turned into a 10-mile adventure because I couldn't get myself to turn around. When I would get back to the car, my stomach would be furiously growling because I didn't bring anything to eat. I would be ravenous and I'd dig in the glove box for my emergency stash of protein bars. Having spent so many days starving outside, I have learned that it's really beneficial to bring along some snacks so I can make my day last even longer. Then I'm the one who can decide when it's time to go in, not my stomach.

Now, anytime I leave the house, I make sure my pockets are full of high-protein homemade snacks like my Roasted Rosemary Sage Almonds (page 81) or Summit Bars (page 90). I can snack on these kinds of packable foods throughout the day, and they keep my hunger at bay while I explore the endless terrain around the Eastern Sierra. All the recipes in this chapter are easy to prepare ahead of time, and they are even easier to wrap up and take with you. They are also effortless and flavorful snacks to have on hand in your pantry. For that reason, these are some of my favorite recipes to make. — KIMMY

Roasted Rosemary Sage Almonds

Makes 1 pound

These almonds are my lifesaver for traveling and hiking adventures. They also
make a seemingly fancy snack with little effort for a houseful of guests. Give your
normal bowl of nuts a fresh makeover. — KIMMY

3 tablespoons (45 ml) olive oil

2 tablespoons (4 g) fresh rosemary,
destemmed and chopped

1 tablespoon (1 g) chopped
fresh sage leaves

½ teaspoon cayenne pepper

¼ teaspoon lemon zest

¼ teaspoon fine sea salt

1 pound (454 g) raw whole
almonds with their skins

1 tablespoon (15 ml)
fresh lemon juice

¼ teaspoon coarse sea salt

~~~~ SEA LEVEL ~~~~

Follow the recipe as noted.

Preheat the oven to 300°F. Line a baking sheet with parchment
paper.

In a large frying pan, heat the olive oil on medium heat. Add
the rosemary, sage, cayenne, lemon zest, and sea salt. Cook on
medium heat for 1 to 3 minutes. The herbs and zest will smell
fragrant. Add the almonds and sauté until they are coated. Add
the lemon juice and cook for 1 minute.

Remove the almonds from the heat and transfer them to the
prepared baking sheet. Bake for 10 minutes, remove the almonds
and stir, and bake again for an additional 10 minutes.

Remove the almonds from the oven and immediately sprinkle
them with the sea salt. Allow to cool completely on the baking
sheet. Serve, once cooled to room temperature.

Store in an airtight container for up to 1 month.

Honey Roasted Peanuts

Makes 1 pound

Honey roasted peanuts have always been one of my go-to snacks.
They're sweet, salty, and also have protein. What more could you want?
When I lived in Vermont at boarding school, my mom would send me care
packages with my grandma's bread and a big tub of honey roasted peanuts.
Now that I'm in charge of making my own snacks, I have created my own
and keep these peanuts in my pantry at all times. — MIMI

1 pound (454 g) raw peanuts
with their skins

2 tablespoons (28 g) salted butter

¼ cup (85 g) raw honey

¼ cup (57 g) cane sugar

½ teaspoon fine sea salt

TOPPING

¼ cup plus 2 tablespoons
(85 g) cane sugar

1 teaspoon fine sea salt

SEA LEVEL

Follow the recipe as noted.

Preheat the oven to 300°F. Line a baking sheet with parchment
paper. In a large bowl, add the peanuts and set aside.

In a medium saucepan, add the butter, honey, ¼ cup cane sugar,
and ½ teaspoon sea salt and melt over medium heat. When the
sugar is completely dissolved, remove from the heat. Pour the
sugar mixture over the peanuts and stir to coat completely.

Transfer the peanut mixture to the prepared baking sheet and
spread out evenly. Bake for 35 minutes, stirring halfway through.

To make the topping: In a small dish, add together the ¼ cup
plus 2 tablespoons cane sugar and 1 teaspoon sea salt and mix
together. Sprinkle over the top of the warm peanuts and stir to
coat completely. Let cool completely on the baking sheet.

Store in an airtight container for 1 month.

Sweet & Salty Trail Mix

Makes 6 cups

Having something like trail mix is handy for more than just hiking. When I'm at the bake shop, sometimes I need a quick snack to keep me going before I can take time for a meal. This trail mix has protein from nuts, energy from dried fruits, and chocolate—well, just because. The best part about making your own trail mix is that you can switch up the ingredients with whatever dried fruit or nuts you have in your pantry. If you're out of one of the ingredients listed here, try mixing in something new. —MIMI

2 cups (425 g) Sunspire SunDrops

1 cup (127 g) pecan halves

1 cup (142 g) roasted and salted peanuts

1 cup (170 g) dried blueberries

1 cup (127 g) dried cranberries

·········· VEGAN ··········

Replace the SunDrops with dark chocolate chunks.

〰〰 SEA LEVEL 〰〰

Follow the recipe as noted.

In a medium mixing bowl, add all the ingredients. Mix together until combined.

Store in an airtight container for up to 1 month.

Mountain Trail Mix

Makes 5 cups

Hunza raisins are a variety of raisin that is similar in taste and flavor to golden raisins. They have a leafy green color and are grown at an altitude of 6,000 to 9,000 feet. Because they are grown so high in altitude, they get their irrigation from melting mountain spring water. If you can't find them, another variety of raisins will work. If you can get them, I highly recommend it, as they are a unique ingredient that will make your trail mix stand out from the rest. — MIMI

1 cup (155 g) Hunza raisins

1 cup (213 g) dark chocolate covered raisins

1 cup (142 g) whole raw almonds

1 cup (142 g) roasted and salted cashews (whole or pieces)

1 cup (170 g) white chocolate chunks

SEA LEVEL

Follow the recipe as noted.

In a large bowl, mix all the ingredients together.

Store in an airtight container for up to 1 month.

Savory Trail Mix

Makes 5½ cups

Roasted Rosemary Sage Almonds (page 81) are something I always search for in Kimmy's pantry when I'm waiting for dinner to be done. They fill me up just enough. So I decided to create a trail mix with them while also adding some of my other favorite things. The toasted coconut gives this trail mix a little sweetness without taking away from the savory side that many trail mixes lack. —MIMI

2 cups (127 g) unsweetened wide flake coconut

1½ cups (213 g) Roasted Rosemary Sage Almonds (page 81)

1 cup (142 g) roasted, salted, and shelled pistachios

1 cup (57 g) pretzel twists

Preheat the oven to 350°F. Line a baking sheet with parchment paper. Spread the coconut onto the prepared baking sheet. Bake for 5 minutes, or until golden brown. Allow to cool completely on the baking sheet.

In a large bowl, mix all the ingredients together.

Store in an airtight container for up to 1 month.

·········· GLUTEN-FREE ··········

Use gluten-free pretzels.

〜〜〜 SEA LEVEL 〜〜〜

Follow the recipe as noted.

Summit Bars

Makes 9 bars

I wanted to create a snack that wasn't just another granola bar. I thought of the things that would be sweet but also help sustain me when I'm outdoors. I chose chocolate chips, blueberries, and almonds because they are my favorites. You can use them or replace them with your favorites. You'll probably want to bake these for more than just adventuring outside. —MIMI

½ cup (113 g) salted butter, softened

½ cup (113 g) cane sugar

¼ cup (57 g) packed dark brown sugar

1 teaspoon vanilla extract

2 large eggs

¼ cup (64 g) almond butter

1½ cups (191 g) all-purpose flour

½ teaspoon baking soda

½ teaspoon fine sea salt

½ cup (99 g) semi-sweet chocolate chips

½ cup (85 g) dried blueberries

½ cup (57 g) sliced almonds with their skins

2 tablespoons (21 g) flaxseeds

.... GLUTEN-FREE ....

Replace the all-purpose flour with 1¼ cups plus 1 tablespoon (205 g) gluten-free flour blend.

〰〰〰 SEA LEVEL 〰〰〰

Bake at 325°F for 32 minutes, or until a toothpick inserted in the center comes out clean.

Preheat the oven to 325°F. Line a 9-by-9-inch baking pan with parchment paper.

In the bowl of a stand mixer fitted with the paddle attachment, add the butter, cane sugar, dark brown sugar, and vanilla extract. Mix on low until combined and no chunks of butter remain. Add the eggs and almond butter, mix on low for three to four rotations. Do not overmix.

In a separate bowl, add the flour, baking soda, and sea salt and whisk together. Add to the butter mixture and mix on low until a stiff dough forms.

In a separate bowl, add the chocolate chips, blueberries, almonds, and flaxseeds and mix to combine. Add about three-quarters of the mixture into the dough and mix on low until combined.

Press the dough into the prepared pan so it is evenly dispersed. Sprinkle the remaining chocolate chip mixture on top of the dough.

Bake for 28 minutes, or until a toothpick inserted in the center comes out clean. Allow to cool completely. Remove the bars from the pan and cut into nine squares.

Store in an airtight container for up to 7 days.

Walnut Oat Bars

Makes 9 bars

For most of my adult life, I have dabbled with gluten-free recipes because at times my body feels sluggish when wheat is consistently in my diet. Oats have become my common replacement for wheat, and these incredible oat bars are great for mornings on the go or as a packable snack. They are dense and full of goodness. This dough also makes great cookie dough, so if you don't have time to bake it, form it into 12 balls and then freeze on a cookie sheet for a sweet treat for later. — KIMMY

3½ cups (349 g) rolled oats

1½ teaspoons baking powder

1 teaspoon fine sea salt

¼ teaspoon cinnamon

2 cups (226 g) walnuts

3 tablespoons (45 ml) canola oil

¾ cup (238 g) agave

¼ cup (60 ml) warm water

2 teaspoons vanilla extract

¾ cup (106 g) dark chocolate chunks

·········· GLUTEN-FREE ··········

Use gluten-free oats.

〜〜〜 SEA LEVEL 〜〜〜

Bake at 350°F for 25 to 30 minutes, or until lightly golden brown.

Preheat the oven to 350°F. Line a 9-by-9-inch baking pan with parchment paper.

In a food processor, process 1½ cups of the oats until ground into a fine flour. Add to a medium mixing bowl with the baking powder, sea salt, and cinnamon and whisk together. Set aside.

In the food processor (no need to wash), grind the walnuts until ground into fine pieces. Add the canola oil and blend for 30 seconds to 1 minute, or until it's a nut butter consistency. Scrape the sides and blend for another 30 seconds to incorporate completely. Set aside.

In a medium bowl, whisk together the agave and warm water. Add the walnut butter mixture and vanilla extract to the agave mixture. Whisk together until combined and allow to sit for 3 minutes. Add the walnut butter mixture to the ground oat mixture and whisk together until combined. Using a spatula, fold in the remaining 2 cups of the rolled oats and the dark chocolate chunks.

Transfer the batter into the prepared pan. Using the spatula, spread out and press into the pan evenly. Bake for 18 to 20 minutes, or until lightly golden brown. Let cool completely in the baking pan. Once cool, cut into nine bars.

Store in an airtight container for up to 7 days.

Chewy Granola Bars

Makes 18 bars

When I was snowboarding all the time, I always kept chewy granola bars in my jacket pocket. They were the perfect snack while I was on the hill, and they were healthier than anything I could find at the lodge. This recipe is a flavor I have always wanted to see in a commercially made granola bar, but now I just make my own. — MIMI

3 cups (298 g) rolled oats

1 cup (85 g) finely shredded unsweetened coconut

½ teaspoon fine sea salt

½ cup (113 g) cane sugar

3 tablespoons (64 g) raw honey

¼ cup (57 g) coconut oil

¼ cup (57 g) salted butter

1 teaspoon vanilla extract

1½ cups (7½ ounces; 212 g) finely chopped milk chocolate

············· GLUTEN-FREE ·············

Use gluten-free oats.

〰〰〰 SEA LEVEL 〰〰〰

Bake at 350°F for 11 minutes, remove from oven and stir, then bake again for 11 more minutes, or until golden brown.

Preheat the oven to 350°F. Line a baking sheet with parchment paper and spread the oats evenly onto the paper. Bake for 10 minutes, remove from oven, and stir. Bake again for 10 more minutes, until golden brown. Allow to cool.

In a large mixing bowl, add the oats, coconut, and sea salt. Stir to combine completely. Set aside.

Line a 9-by-13-inch baking pan with parchment paper. In a small saucepan, add the cane sugar, honey, coconut oil, and butter. Heat on medium heat until completely melted. Once bubbling, let it simmer for about 1 minute. Remove from the heat.

Pour the hot sugar mixture over the oat mixture and fold a few times. Then add in the vanilla extract and continue to mix until completely combined.

Transfer the mixture into the prepared baking pan and press to evenly distribute. Allow the mixture to cool completely, about 6 hours or overnight.

Cut around the edges and remove entirely from the pan. Cut lengthwise down the middle, then cut each side into nine bars.

To temper the chocolate: Place about 80 percent of the chocolate in a heatproof bowl and set aside the remaining 20 percent. To create a double boiler, fill a small saucepan with water and place the bowl with the 80 percent of the chocolate on top; do not let the bowl touch the water. Turn on to high heat and melt the chocolate until it reaches 110°F on a digital thermometer. Remove from the heat. Immediately add in the remaining 20 percent of chocolate and stir vigorously to combine completely. Allow the chocolate to come down to 89°F.

Test to see if the chocolate is tempered by placing a bit on a piece of parchment paper, and then stick it in the freezer for 1 to 2 minutes. Remove it and if the chocolate looks shinyand snaps, it's all set. If not, you can reheat the chocolate and add in a little more finely chopped chocolate to start the process again.

Line a baking sheet with parchment paper, dip the bottoms of each bar into the melted chocolate, and place chocolate side down on the baking sheet. Place baking sheet in the fridge to set, about 1 hour.

Store in a cool, dry place for up to 2 weeks.

Chocolate Peanut Butter Mendiants

Makes 20 mendiants

Mendiants are a traditional French candy. They are little disks of chocolate topped with dried fruits and nuts. I like to think of these as packable fuel. When you mix dark chocolate and peanut butter together, you get a little protein plus some sweet and salty goodness that can keep you going until you get home. — MIMI

1¼ cups (5 ounces; 142 g) finely chopped dark chocolate

¼ cup (71 g) peanut butter

Scant ¼ cup (30 g) roasted and salted peanuts, coarsely chopped

～～～～ SEA LEVEL ～～～～

Follow the recipe as noted.

Line two baking sheets with parchment paper.

Temper the chocolate using the instructions on page 95.

Once the chocolate is tempered, add in the peanut butter and stir to combine completely. Scoop 1 scant tablespoon of the chocolate–peanut butter mixture onto the parchment paper to form a round disk of chocolate. Top with chopped peanuts. Repeat until all the chocolate–peanut butter mixture and peanuts are gone. Place the tray in the fridge to set, about 1 hour.

Store in a cool, dry place or in the fridge for up to 2 weeks.

Cashew Clusters

Makes 24 clusters

I've always preferred butterscotch to caramel, so while most people make the ever-so-popular turtle candies with pecans, caramel, and chocolate—I make these cashew clusters with chewy butterscotch, cashews, and pretzels. Make these ahead of time so that you can easily pop them in your pocket for outdoor adventures. — MIMI

¾ cup (170 g) cane sugar

1 teaspoon blackstrap molasses

¼ cup (57 grams) salted butter

½ cup (120 ml) heavy
  whipping cream

½ teaspoon vanilla extract

¼ teaspoon fine sea salt,
  more for topping

Heaping 1½ cups (226 g)
  roasted and salted cashews
  (whole or halves)

1⅓ cups (113 g) pretzels,
  chopped into pieces about
  the size of cashews

3 cups plus 3 tablespoons
  (16 ounces; 454 g) finely
  chopped milk chocolate

············ GLUTEN-FREE ············

Use gluten-free pretzels.

〰〰〰 SEA LEVEL 〰〰〰

Follow the recipe as noted.

Line a baking sheet with parchment paper. Set aside.

In a medium saucepan, cook the sugar and molasses over medium heat. Stir so the sugar doesn't burn and until the mixture has become smooth with no remaining clumps.

Once the sugar mixture is smooth, carefully add the butter while stirring constantly, so the butter doesn't burn. When combined, carefully add in the cream in small increments while continuing to stir until completely combined. Remove from the heat.

Add in the vanilla extract and ¼ teaspoon sea salt and stir to combine completely. Add the cashews and pretzels to the saucepan and stir to combine them completely.

Using a spoon, drop clusters of the cashew mixture onto the prepared baking sheet. Put the baking sheet in the freezer. This will help them stay together when they are dipped in chocolate.

Temper the chocolate using the instructions on page 95.

Remove the baking sheet from the freezer and dip each cashew cluster in the melted chocolate. Place them back on the baking sheet. Put the baking sheet in the fridge to set for about 1 hour. Sprinkle the clusters with sea salt (optional).

Store in a cool, dry place, or in the fridge for up to 2 weeks.

APRÈS

I have stood on countless mountaintops in Austria, Italy, Germany, and Switzerland and, without looking at my watch, I have known the time by the sound of music pouring out of the resort lodges. Around 3 p.m., each place has the same end-of-day tradition—après. This simple word means *after* in French, and in the world of skiing and snowboarding it's a term that describes a way to relax and replenish after a day outside on the mountain.

Rumor has it that the term *après-ski* was invented in Arlberg, Austria. I will always remember my first trip to this seemingly sleepy town. It was a small resort village, tucked up a windy mountain road that transformed from quaint and quiet to drunken debauchery in a matter of minutes when après hour rolled around. All the mountain enthusiasts let loose on their cozy little sundecks and celebrated a great day in the Austrian Alps.

I admittedly took part in these traditional afternoon festivities, and I always looked forward to the deliciously satisfying small plates of food that were served. Our table was full of small salads, pastries, fries, and cheese plates, and it was enough nourishment to hold me over until dinner. This tradition inspired me to create my own kind of après when I was no longer in the Alps. My friends and family call me the Queen of Après, because when I'm home I'm usually whipping up some kind of snack in my own kitchen. To me, there's nothing better than setting out delicious food for people to snack on all afternoon.

The recipe ideas for this chapter represent a creative expansion on our own versions of après. Whereas I have drawn on my experience of the traditional European après, Mimi has drawn on experiences that are closer to home, like when she would come back from snowboarding to find that her mom's Potato Chips & Onion Dip (page 119) were ready to be devoured. There's no wrong way to enjoy après; it's all about eating food and relaxing in the afternoon after a day outside. The recipes in this chapter will hold you and your friends over until your next meal. Whether it's Basil Caprese Guacamole (page 115) or colorful Fiesta Black Bean Salad (page 108), it's always a good day to après. —KIMMY

Sea Salt Thyme Biscotti

Makes 18 biscotti

Biscotti are usually sweet, but that doesn't mean they can't be savory. This
après snack is a little bit of both—sweet and salty. I like to serve these with
Colby Jack cheese and Fuji apples. —MIMI

½ cup (113 g) salted
  butter, softened

½ cup (113 g) cane sugar

1 teaspoon fresh lemon juice

2 large eggs

1½ cups (255 g) whole wheat flour

1 teaspoon thyme

½ teaspoon sea salt, plus
  extra for dusting

.... GLUTEN-FREE ....

Replace the whole wheat flour with
1¾ cups (269 g) gluten-free flour blend.

〜〜〜〜 SEA LEVEL 〜〜〜〜

Bake at 350°F for 35 minutes, or until the
dough looks set but not completely done.
Remove from the oven and let rest for
10 minutes. Cut as instructed and bake
again for 20 minutes, or until they look
set and dried.

Preheat the oven to 350°F. Line a baking sheet with parchment paper.

In the bowl of a stand mixer fitted with the paddle attachment, add the butter, cane sugar, and lemon juice. Mix on low until combined and no chunks of butter remain. Add the eggs and mix just slightly, enough to break the yolks.

In a separate bowl, add the flour, thyme, and ½ teaspoon sea salt and whisk together. Add the flour mixture to the butter mixture and mix on low until combined into a stiff dough.

Turn the dough out onto the baking sheet and form a log that is about 12-by-2½ inches. Bake for 30 minutes, or until the dough looks set but not completely done. Remove from the oven and let rest for 10 minutes.

To cut: Using a serrated knife (because the biscotti are fragile), trim off the edges, and cut into 18 slices. Space them 1 inch apart on the baking sheet.

Bake again for 15 minutes or until they look set and dried. Sprinkle with sea salt immediately after they come out of the oven. Let cool completely on the baking sheet.

Store in a cool, dry place for up to 7 days.

Rosemary Parmesan Biscotti

Makes 18 biscotti

These little savory biscotti remind me of cheese crackers, but with a lighter texture, thanks to the Parmesan. This biscotti can be baked ahead of time, so it is ready for après the next day. — MIMI

½ cup (113 grams) salted butter, softened

1 cup (64 g) grated Parmesan

3 tablespoons (43 g) cane sugar

2 large eggs

2 cups (255 g) all-purpose flour

2 teaspoons rosemary

1½ teaspoons baking powder

½ teaspoon fine sea salt

·············· GLUTEN-FREE ··············

Replace the all-purpose flour with 1¾ cups (269 g) gluten-free flour blend.

〜〜〜 SEA LEVEL 〜〜〜

Bake at 350°F for 35 minutes, or until the dough looks set but not completely done. Remove from the oven and let rest for 10 minutes. Cut as instructed and bake again for 20 minutes, or until they look set and dried.

Preheat the oven to 350°F. Line a baking sheet with parchment paper.

In the bowl of a stand mixer fitted with the paddle attachment, add the butter, Parmesan, and cane sugar. Mix on low until combined and no chunks of butter remain. Add the eggs and mix just slightly, enough to break the yolks.

In a separate bowl, add the flour, rosemary, baking powder, and sea salt and whisk together. Add the flour mixture to the butter mixture and mix on low until combined into a stiff dough.

Turn the dough out onto the baking sheet and form a log that is about 12-by-2½ inches. Bake for 30 minutes, or until the dough looks set but not completely done. Remove from the oven and let rest for 10 minutes.

To cut: Using a serrated knife (because the biscotti are fragile), trim off the edges, and cut into 18 slices. Space them 1 inch apart on the baking sheet.

Bake again for 15 minutes, or until they look set and dried. Let cool completely on the baking sheet.

Store in a cool, dry place for up to 7 days.

Strawberry Walnut Salad

Makes 4 servings

When I was a little girl, I loved gardening with my mom. One of my favorite things was picking out the biggest and juiciest strawberries. I could tell which ones they were from their bright red color, and I would eat a few right off the plant as I gathered the others. Even though a salad is a pretty basic dish, it's helpful to have a delicious and reliable go-to that can be quickly assembled for an unexpected full house of guests. I make my own dressing, and the refreshing and delicious caramelized red onions are the perfect complement to this otherwise simple salad. The best thing about the dressing is that you can use it on any salad you like! — **KIMMY**

SALAD

1 tablespoon (14 g) coconut oil

¾ cup (140 g) sliced red onion

2 teaspoons balsamic vinegar

4 cups (168 g) baby spinach

2 cups (70 g) mixed baby greens

8 large strawberries, quartered

1 medium avocado, cubed

Heaping ½ cup (57 g) walnut pieces

¼ cup (35 g) packed
crumbled goat cheese

2 tablespoons (20 g) hemp seeds

DRESSING

3 tablespoons (45 ml) olive oil

2 tablespoons (43 g) raw honey

2 tablespoons (30 ml)
balsamic vinegar

1 tablespoon (15 ml) fresh lemon juice

1 teaspoon apple cider vinegar

2 teaspoons nutritional yeast

1 teaspoons basil

1 teaspoon thyme

1 teaspoon oregano

⅛ teaspoon fine sea salt

⅛ teaspoon black pepper

In a small frying pan on medium heat, melt the coconut oil. Add the sliced red onion and cook for 2 to 3 minutes, until it becomes translucent. Add 2 teaspoons of the balsamic vinegar. Stir and cook on medium heat for 1 minute more. Remove from the heat.

To make the dressing: In a sealable jar, add the olive oil, honey, 2 tablespoons balsamic vinegar, lemon juice, and apple cider vinegar.

In a small bowl, mix together the nutritional yeast, basil, thyme, oregano, sea salt, and pepper. Pour the dry ingredients into the sealable jar and shake until combined thoroughly.

To make the salad: In a medium salad bowl, layer the spinach, baby greens, strawberries, avocado, walnuts, and goat cheese. Add the cooked red onions, and sprinkle the hemp seeds on top. Drizzle the dressing over the top and toss the salad just before serving.

Store any extra dressing in the fridge for up to 3 days.

〰〰〰 **SEA LEVEL** 〰〰〰

Follow the recipe as noted.

Fiesta Black Bean Salad

Makes 6 cups

This colorful black bean salad is easy to prepare ahead of a busy weekend, and it makes a perfect side dish for friendly gatherings. My "secret" ingredient is the mango, which gives the salad a sweet and unique flavor. Make this into a meal by simply heating it on the stovetop for 5 to 8 minutes, and then rolling it up in tortillas for delicious burritos. — KIMMY

SALAD

Two 15-ounce cans (850 g) black beans, drained and rinsed

2 cups (372 g) fresh or canned corn

1 medium mango, peeled and chopped

1 small red onion, diced

1 medium red pepper, deseeded and diced

⅓ cup (7 g) roughly chopped fresh cilantro

1 medium avocado, diced

DRESSING

⅓ cup (80 ml) fresh lime juice

3 tablespoons (45 ml) olive oil

1 tablespoon (15 ml) apple cider vinegar

1 teaspoon nutritional yeast

1 teaspoon raw honey

½ teaspoon chili powder

½ teaspoon garlic powder

SEA LEVEL

Follow the recipe as noted.

To make the salad: In a large bowl, add the black beans, corn, mango, red onion, red pepper, and cilantro. Mix thoroughly. (Don't add the avocado until the salad is ready to be served to avoid the natural browning process.)

To make the dressing: Add all the dressing ingredients to a food processor and blend for 30 seconds. Scrape down the sides and bottom, and blend for 1 minute. Pour the dressing over the salad 30 to 45 minutes prior to serving to marinate. Stir a couple times to ensure it's well seasoned. Store the salad in the fridge, covered, until time to serve.

Just before serving, add the avocado and give the salad one more stir.

Store in the fridge for up to 3 days.

Greek Pasta Salad

Makes 6 servings

Growing up, we had a salad along with dinner every single night, and a lot of the time it was a Greek salad. My dad, however, was a strong believer in never buying crumbled feta, even if he was going to crumble it for the salad anyway. He always said that true Greeks use block or chunk feta and crumble it themselves. So, that's what I do. A block or chunk of feta has more flavor than the crumbled variety, and it makes this dish way better than your average salad. Add some chicken or steak to make it into a meal. — MIMI

DRESSING

2 teaspoons oregano

1½ teaspoons fine sea salt

1 teaspoon black pepper

¼ teaspoon garlic powder

¼ teaspoon onion powder

½ cup (120 ml) olive oil

¼ cup (60 ml) balsamic vinegar

1 tablespoon (15 ml)
fresh lemon juice

SALAD

½ pound (226 g) rotini noodles

1 teaspoon fine sea salt

6 ounces (170 g) cherry
tomatoes, quartered

1 large cucumber, sliced
and quartered

⅓ cup (40 g) diced red onion

3 cups (80 g) destemmed,
loosely chopped kale

1 cup (170 g) pitted Kalamata olives

4 ounces (113 g) block feta cheese

.... GLUTEN-FREE ....
Use gluten-free noodles.

⌣⌣⌣ SEA LEVEL ⌣⌣⌣
Follow the recipe as noted.

To make the dressing: In a medium bowl, add the oregano, 1½ teaspoons sea salt, black pepper, garlic powder, and onion powder. Whisk together. Add the olive oil, balsamic vinegar, and lemon juice and whisk to combine completely. Cover and let sit in the fridge overnight.

In a 4-quart pot, boil 2 quarts water. Once boiling, add the noodles and 1 teaspoon sea salt. Cook the noodles until done, for 8 to 10 minutes or the time specified on the package. Strain the noodles and transfer back to pot. Allow the noodles to cool to room temperature before mixing the salad. Or you can make the noodles the night before along with dressing and store in fridge in an airtight container.

To assemble the salad: In a large bowl, add the noodles, cherry tomatoes, cucumber pieces, red onion, kale, and olives. Crumble the feta into the bowl and dress with the salad dressing.

Store in the fridge for up to 5 days.

Baked Brussels Sprouts with Sweet Chili Sauce

Makes 14 ounces Brussels sprouts and 1½ cups sauce

Brussels sprouts have made a major comeback in my kitchen. My first experience with Brussels sprouts was an unappealing steamed version that lacked crispiness and flavor. My mother-in-law made me a roasted version with sweet chili sauce, and my taste buds were transformed! Flavorful and roasted to perfection, these Brussels sprouts are great for dinner parties or as a side dish for any occasion.—KIMMY

SWEET CHILI SAUCE

1 cup (226 g) cane sugar

¾ cup (180 ml) white vinegar

½ cup plus 1½ tablespoons
  (140 ml) water

1 medium carrot, grated

2 tablespoons (33 g) Sambal Oelek
  chili paste, more if desired

3 cloves garlic, crushed
  and left whole

⅛ teaspoon fine sea salt

2 tablespoons (14 g) cornstarch

BRUSSELS SPROUTS

1 tablespoon (14 g) coconut oil

14 ounces (397 g) Brussels sprouts

½ teaspoon fine sea salt

¼ teaspoon black pepper

¼ teaspoon paprika

¼ teaspoon garlic powder

3 tablespoons (43 g)
  Sweet Chili Sauce

1 tablespoon (14 g) tamari
  or soy sauce

〰〰〰 SEA LEVEL 〰〰〰
Bake at 375°F for 40 to 45 minutes, and
return to the oven for 5 to 10 minutes.

Preheat the oven to 375°F.

To make the sauce: In a medium saucepan, combine the cane sugar, vinegar, ½ cup water, carrot, chili paste, garlic, and ⅛ teaspoon sea salt. Bring to a boil and stir occasionally. Boil for about 3 minutes.

While these ingredients are boiling, in a small bowl whisk together the cornstarch and 1½ tablespoons water. Slowly pour the cornstarch mixture into the sugar mixture. Stir to combine and reduce the heat to a low boil. Allow it to boil for about 2 more minutes. Stir occasionally, then remove from the heat. Taste and add more chili paste if desired. Remove and discard the garlic cloves.

To make the Brussels sprouts: Grease a 9-by-9-inch baking dish with the coconut oil and set aside. Rinse the Brussels sprouts, remove the ends, and cut each sprout lengthwise in half. Set aside.

In a small mixing bowl, whisk together the ½ teaspoon sea salt, pepper, paprika, and garlic powder. Set aside.

Add the Brussels sprouts to the prepared baking dish. Sprinkle the whisked seasoning/spices on the Brussels sprouts and stir to ensure they are evenly coated. Place in the oven for 25 to 30 minutes, stirring occasionally, until leaves are brown and crispy. Remove from oven.

In a small dish, whisk together 3 tablespoons of the Sweet Chili Sauce and the tamari, and drizzle over the top of the hot Brussels sprouts and coat evenly. Return them to the oven for an additional 5 to 8 minutes, until slightly caramelized.

Store in an airtight container in the fridge for up to 5 days.

Basil Caprese Guacamole

Makes 4 cups

I love avocado and I love caprese salads, so I thought, why not combine my favorite
ingredients from both to make a delicious dip that goes great with chips, crackers,
and veggies? The fresh basil and chunks of mozzarella with a hint of white balsamic
give this guacamole its own special twist. — **KIMMY**

3 large avocados

1 medium tomato, diced

¼ cup (30 g) diced red onion

2 tablespoons (5 g) finely
  chopped fresh basil

1 garlic clove, diced

1 tablespoon (15 ml) white
  balsamic vinegar

1 tablespoon (15 ml) fresh lime juice

½ teaspoon fine sea salt

½ ball (4 ounces; 113 g)
  fresh mozzarella, cubed

4 to 6 fresh basil leaves for garnish

White corn chips for serving

〰〰〰 SEA LEVEL 〰〰〰
Follow the recipe as noted.

In a medium bowl, mash the avocados using a fork. Stir in the
tomato, red onion, basil, and garlic. Pour in the balsamic vinegar,
lime juice, and sea salt. Mix generously.

Prior to serving, add the cubed mozzarella and garnish with fresh
basil leaves. Serve with white corn chips.

Store in the fridge for up to 2 days.

Lemon Tahini Kale Chips

Makes 6 servings

My mother-in-law introduced me to kale about 10 years ago. She would sauté it, mix it into hearty soups, and make it into chips. I was always amazed at how savory and adaptable these leafy greens were. When I started playing with flavors of my own, I came up with this recipe, which satisfies both the savory and crunchy palette. I even use these chips as garnishes for soups, as a topping for salads, and as a crispy element in my sandwiches. Every time I make them I have people asking me for the recipe, so here it is. — **KIMMY**

2 large bunches (200 g) kale, leaves destemmed

2 tablespoons (32 g) tahini

2 tablespoons (30 ml) fresh lemon juice

1½ tablespoons (10 g) nutritional yeast

1 tablespoon (15 ml) water

¼ teaspoon garlic powder

¼ teaspoon turmeric

¼ teaspoon cayenne pepper

¼ teaspoon fine sea salt

〰〰〰 SEA LEVEL 〰〰〰

Bake at 250°F for 30 minutes. Rotate the pans and lightly toss kale to bake evenly. Bake for 20 to 25 more minutes, or until the kale is crispy and slightly golden brown.

Preheat the oven to 250°F. Line two baking sheets with parchment paper.

Rinse and thoroughly dry the kale. Make sure the leaves have no stems, and then tear each into palm size or smaller pieces. Add the kale to a large mixing bowl and set aside.

In a food processor combine the tahini, lemon juice, nutritional yeast, water, garlic powder, turmeric, cayenne, and sea salt. Blend for 30 seconds. Scrape the sides and base, and blend again for 1 minute or until creamy and smooth.

Add the tahini mixture to the kale and toss thoroughly, using your hands to coat the leaves evenly. Pinch the tahini mixture into the leaves to avoid large clumps of sauce on the kale. Spread the kale mixture thinly onto the prepared baking sheets; try to avoid overlapping the kale leaves to ensure even baking.

Bake for 25 minutes. Rotate the pans and lightly toss the kale to bake evenly. Bake for 15 to 20 minutes more, or until the kale is crispy and slightly golden brown. If some of the chips are still wet with the seasoning, remove crispy pieces and allow remaining pieces to get crispy. Remove from the oven and let cool completely on baking sheets.

Store in an airtight container for 7 days.

Potato Chips & Onion Dip

Makes 4 servings

One of my mom's favorite après snacks is potato chips (heavy on the salt) and onion dip. She always had chips in the cupboard, and she made onion dip from scratch. In the spring, after skiing, she would have it ready and waiting for us when we got home. I have upgraded this snack by making my own chips—it's so easy to do and totally worth it! The best part is that you can make them ahead of time and they last for days (unless you eat them all first). And, Mom—you can add as much salt as you want. —MIMI

POTATO CHIPS

1 medium potato

1½ tablespoons (22 ml) avocado oil

1 teaspoon cornstarch

Fine sea salt

ONION DIP

1 cup (8 ounces; 226 g) sour cream

2 heaping tablespoons chopped
fresh chives

2 teaspoons Everything
Spice Mix (page 29)

1 teaspoon fresh lemon juice

················· VEGAN ·················

Use vegan sour cream.

〰〰〰 SEA LEVEL 〰〰〰

Bake at 325°F for 50 minutes to 1 hour,
or until golden brown.

Preheat the oven to 325°F. Line two baking sheets with parchment paper.

To make the potato chips: Using a mandoline, slice the potato into ⅛-inch slices. Soak the slices in a medium bowl with 2 cups cold water. Let sit for 10 to 20 minutes, until the water looks murky. This removes the starch and will help get a crispier chip. When done soaking, drain the potato slices.

In a medium bowl, combine the avocado oil and cornstarch. Add the potato slices to the bowl and coat completely with the avocado oil–cornstarch mixture. Lay each potato slice flat on the prepared baking sheets. Do not overlap the potatoes or they will not cook properly.

Bake for 40 to 50 minutes, or until golden brown. Remove from the oven and immediately sprinkle with the sea salt on top of the chips so it sticks.

To make the onion dip: In a medium bowl, add all the ingredients. Stir to combine completely.

Store the chips in an airtight container for up to 2 weeks and store the dip in the fridge for up to 7 days.

Zucchini Chips & Hummus

Makes 4 to 6 servings

One of my guilty pleasures is chips and hummus, so I'm always looking for healthy alternatives for chips. These zucchini chips are the perfect combination of garlic and cheesy goodness, and they have a crisp finish that satisfies my desire for chips. Pair them with this hummus (it is always in my fridge) and you have a satisfying snack. —KIMMY

CHIPS

1 pound (454 g) zucchinis

1 tablespoon plus ¼ teaspoon fine sea salt

¼ cup (16 g) finely grated Parmesan

3 garlic cloves, minced

1 teaspoon apple cider vinegar

HUMMUS

¼ cup (64 g) tahini

¼ cup fresh lemon juice (about 1 medium lemon)

2 tablespoons (30 ml) olive oil

2 small garlic cloves, minced

½ teaspoon cumin

½ teaspoon fine sea salt

One 8.8-ounce can (250 g) cooked chickpeas, drained and rinsed

2 to 3 tablespoons water

¼ teaspoon paprika for topping

.... VEGAN ....

Substitute the Parmesan for a vegan Parmesan.

〜〜〜 SEA LEVEL 〜〜〜

Bake at 200°F for 3½ to 4½ hours, or until golden brown and crispy. Rotate the trays every 30 to 45 minutes and move the chips from the middle to the edges for even browning.

Preheat the oven to 200°F. Line two baking sheets with parchment paper.

To make the chips: Using a mandoline, slice each zucchini longways into ¼-inch slices. Lay the zucchini slices evenly spaced on a clean surface (not on the baking sheets just yet, to avoid moisture on the parchment paper). Lightly sprinkle the 1 tablespoon sea salt over the sliced zucchini to pull moisture out of the zucchini. Let sit for 15 minutes, or until droplets of water are abundant on the tops of the zucchinis.

Using a clean dish towel, pat the zucchini slices dry to absorb the excess moisture, and place in a medium bowl.

In a large bowl, combine the Parmesan, garlic, vinegar, and ¼ teaspoon sea salt. Toss together with your hands to combine. Then add the zucchinis to the bowl and, using your hands, coat them evenly.

Arrange the slices on the prepared baking sheets and bake for 3 to 4 hours, or until golden brown and crispy. Rotate the trays every 30 to 45 minutes and move the chips from the middle to the edges for even browning.

To make the hummus: In a food processor, combine the tahini and lemon juice and process for 1 minute. Scrape down the sides and bottom of the bowl. Process for another 30 seconds. Add the olive oil, garlic, cumin, and ½ teaspoon sea salt to the tahini mixture. Process for 30 seconds, scraping the sides and bottom of the bowl multiple times until well blended.

Add the chickpeas to the food processor and process for 1 minute. Continue to scrape the sides and bottom of the bowl until the mixture is thick and smooth. Add 2 to 3 tablespoons water until you reach the perfect consistency. Sprinkle the hummus with the paprika for serving.

Store the hummus in an airtight container in the fridge for 7 days. Store the chips in an airtight container for 3 days.

Sweet Potato Fries

Makes 4 servings

I have a long-standing relationship with sweet potato fries. They were my weekend indulgence after my ski races when I was little, and they became a weekly tradition as I got older. I have fine-tuned the flavor and crispness of this recipe over the years, and these fries have become a family favorite for every occasion. The secret to this recipe is to add the sea salt as the last step, which guarantees crisp and perfect fries every time. — KIMMY

1 pound (454 g) sweet potatoes

2 tablespoons (14 g) cornstarch

½ teaspoon garlic powder

½ teaspoon cumin

½ teaspoon parsley, plus
  ½ teaspoon for garnish

¼ teaspoon paprika

2 tablespoons (28 g) coconut oil,
  melted

½ teaspoon fine sea salt

〰〰 SEA LEVEL 〰〰

Bake at 425°F for 20 minutes. Flip each fry over and cook for another 10 minutes, or until lightly golden brown.

Peel the sweet potatoes and cut them into ¼-inch-wide long strips. Place the cut sweet potatoes in a bowl of cold water. Soak for 20 minutes until the water looks murky; this removes the starch and will help get a crispier fry.

Preheat the oven to 425°F. Line two baking sheets with parchment paper.

In a small bowl, mix together the cornstarch, garlic powder, cumin, ½ teaspoon parsley, and paprika. Set aside.

Rinse and pat the sweet potatoes dry. Place them in a clean and dry large bowl. Drizzle the melted coconut oil over the sweet potatoes. Slowly sprinkle the seasoning mixture over the potatoes and allow the cornstarch to soak in for a few minutes, until you no longer see powder.

Lay the sweet potato strips out evenly on the parchment paper; do not overlap. Bake for 15 minutes. Flip each strip over and cook for another 10 minutes, or until lightly golden brown.

Remove from the oven and sprinkle with ½ teaspoon sea salt. Allow to cool on the baking sheets for at least 5 to 10 minutes before serving. Garnish with the remaining ½ teaspoon parsley.

Store in an airtight container in the fridge for up to 3 days.

REFRESHMENTS

You may not think of a refreshment as anything more than something to quench your thirst, but they can be a lot more. In fact, refreshments are one of my favorite snacks. Sometimes, slowly savoring or sipping on a drink is even better than indulging in dessert, especially when it's my White Out Shake (page 144). Just like food, refreshments can make memories and transport you to another place and time.

Ingredients really matter for refreshments—whether it's the whiskey for your Hot Toddy (page 136), the red wine for your Glühwein (page 140), or the milk for your Old-Fashioned Hot Cocoa

(page 128). So when you're shopping for ingredients for dinners and desserts, pick up a few extras for refreshments to complete your meal.

Use the recipes in this chapter to elevate other recipes in the book. You can serve Irish Coffee (page 135) with Koloodia Cookies (page 186) for a dessert that you will want to linger over and enjoy (this is the perfect cookie to go with coffee). Or enjoy a Hot Toddy (page 136) with Vanilla Bean Biscotti (page 189) for a heavenly après. Whatever you choose to pair together, the recipes in this chapter will help you create new memories that will be crave-worthy, guaranteed. — MIMI

Sparkling Spring Water

Makes 2 liters

There's a freshwater spring by one of our favorite climbing spots on the way to Yosemite. We stop to fill up jugs of water every time, and Mimi has a SodaStream that she uses to create sparkling water from what we bring back. You've never tasted anything fresher in your life! I love adding fresh fruits to it because it's an easy way to make it interesting without much effort, and there's nothing like a cold glass of it after a long day of climbing. — **KIMMY**

1 medium orange

1 medium lemon

Half a medium cucumber

64 ounces (2 L) sparkling water

Slice the orange and lemon into ¼-inch-thick slices. Slice the cucumber very thin.

In a pitcher, add the sparkling water, ice, orange, lemon, and cucumber.

~~~~~ SEA LEVEL ~~~~~

Follow the recipe as noted.

Old-Fashioned Hot Cocoa

Makes 2 servings

When we opened Dessert'D, one of the first things I knew we would serve was hot chocolate. It has been my favorite drink since I was a child. It is what I craved after a long day of sledding with my friends, and it's what I looked forward to at the end of a cold day skiing. I also knew I wanted our hot cocoa to be different from what was served at most coffee shops: no syrups or bottled sweeteners for us. When I was growing up, I tried "old-fashioned" hot cocoa at my best friend's house. Her dad made hot chocolate for us with milk, sugar, and cocoa. As he swirled the ingredients over an open flame, he told us, "Hot cocoa takes time, it's not instant." I firmly believe that he was right, which is why our recipe is all about letting the true ingredients shine. — MIMI

4 cups (960 ml) milk

2 tablespoons plus 2 teaspoons (39 g) cane sugar

3 tablespoons plus 1 teaspoon (17 g) Dutch cocoa powder

VARIATIONS

Almond: add ½ teaspoon almond flavor

Banana: add ½ teaspoon banana flavor

Cherry: add ½ teaspoon cherry flavor

Peppermint: add ½ teaspoon peppermint flavor

Raspberry: add ½ teaspoon raspberry flavor

TOPPINGS

Whipped Cream (recipe follows)

Vanilla Bean Marshmallows (recipe follows)

In a small saucepan, add the milk, sugar, and cocoa (and flavor if using). Put over high heat.

Stir with a whisk to combine completely until the temperature reaches 140°F on a drink thermometer. Remove from the heat.

Top with Whipped Cream and marshmallows.

VEGAN

Replace the milk with any vegan milk of your choice.

SEA LEVEL

Follow the recipe as noted.

WHIPPED CREAM

Makes 3 cups

2 cups (480 ml) heavy
  whipping cream

1 tablespoon (14 g) cane sugar

1 teaspoon vanilla extract

〰〰〰 SEA LEVEL 〰〰〰

Follow the recipe as noted.

My husband, Delaney, had a special grandma, Phoebe. She used to make him homemade whipped cream when he was young, and when we opened Dessert'D, he wanted to create a whipped cream recipe just like it for us. And we've been making it this way at the bake shop ever since. This whipped cream can be used for so many things: Old-Fashioned Hot Cocoa (page 128), Chocolate Waffles (page 68), Irish Coffee (page 135), and much more! — MIMI

In the bowl of a stand mixer fitted with the whisk attachment, or in a bowl using a hand mixer, add all the ingredients.

Slowly start to mix, so it doesn't splatter, and gradually increase the speed while the mixture thickens until you are at full speed. Whisk until stiff peaks form and the whipped cream doesn't fall off the whisk.

Use immediately, or store in the fridge for up to 7 days.

VANILLA BEAN MARSHMALLOWS

Makes 24 large or 96 mini marshmallows

1 cup cold water

2 tablespoons plus ½ teaspoon
  (22 g) gelatin

2 cups (454 g) cane sugar

1 cup (312 g) light corn syrup

½ teaspoon fine sea salt

1 teaspoon ground vanilla bean

Canola oil spray

Powdered sugar for dusting

〰〰〰 SEA LEVEL 〰〰〰

Follow the recipe as noted.

You just can't have hot cocoa without marshmallows!
Unlike the store-bought kind, these marshmallows are made
without all the additives and such. You can also sandwich
these between Brown Butter Oatmeal Raisin Cookies
(page 177) and light them up them with a kitchen torch for
a rustic dessert. — MIMI

Place a piece of parchment paper in a 9-by-13-inch
baking dish. Let the parchment fold over the dish on two
sides, but make sure the other sides are cut to fit the dish
exactly, otherwise the corners of the marshmallows will
not be perfectly square.

In the bowl of a stand mixer fitted with the whisk
attachment, add ½ cup of the cold water and gelatin.
Immediately stir together with a spoon so it doesn't
clump. Set aside.

In a medium saucepan, add the cane sugar, corn syrup,
the remaining ½ cup water, and sea salt. Put over high
heat and stir with a high heat spatula until all the sugar
has dissolved and you have a liquid. Periodically stir
the sugar mixture until it starts to bubble and rise up.
Remove from the heat and pour directly over the gelatin
in the mixing bowl.

Start mixing on low and gradually increase the speed
as the mixture starts to thicken. It will start out as an
opaque color and slowly it will start to lighten in color
as it thickens. Keep increasing the speed until you are
at full speed.

Continue mixing on high until the mixture is a thick
consistency and resembles marshmallow fluff. It
should be sticky and hold its shape for a short period
of time. The entire mixing time should be about 10 to
15 minutes. Last, add in the vanilla bean and whisk
to combine completely.

Grease the prepared parchment paper and two additional sides of the baking dish with canola oil spray. Immediately pour the marshmallow mixture into the pan. Let the marshmallow set overnight.

On a baking sheet with parchment paper, or a work surface, sift a generous amount of powdered sugar. Slowly pull at the ends of the marshmallow that are not against the parchment paper so it's not stuck to the pan. Lift the entire marshmallow out of the pan and turn it upside down onto the powdered sugar. Sift more powdered sugar on top.

Using a pizza cutter (this is a great trick, but a sharp knife will do as well), cut into 24 squares (six by four). You can leave as large marshmallows or cut each square into four pieces for mini marshmallows.

Roll each side in the powdered sugar to keep from sticking together. Allow them to sit out overnight before storing so the powdered sugar can form to the sides and they won't stick together.

Store in an airtight container for up to 2 weeks.

Irish Coffee

Makes 2 coffees

The first time I had an Irish coffee was actually at the restaurant where Kimmy worked, and she happened to be our server that night. I was finishing up dinner with a few friends when Kimmy delivered this warm, beautiful-looking drink with cream on top to our table. One of my friends had ordered it. I immediately asked what it was, and as he told me he offered to let me taste it. I'm pretty sure I drank more than my fair share of that cocktail! That warm and creamy drink was the perfect ending to our dinner on a cold, snowy night. Now I can make my own at home (and I don't have to share). — MIMI

2 cups (480 ml) brewed coffee

2 tablespoons (30 ml) heavy whipping cream

2 shots Irish whiskey

2 teaspoons King Arthur Flour's Malted Milk Powder

1 tablespoon plus 1 teaspoon (20 g) cane sugar

Whipped Cream (page 131)

~~~~ SEA LEVEL ~~~~

Follow the recipe as noted.

In a small saucepan, add the coffee, whipping cream, Irish whiskey, malted milk powder, and sugar. Heat until it reaches 140°F on a drink thermometer.

Remove from the heat, pour into glasses, and top with Whipped Cream.

Hot Toddy

Makes 2 servings

An evening by the fire is even more relaxing with a hot toddy in hand. I love pairing this warm cocktail with a sweet crunchy cookie, like a Cranberry Orange Ginger Shortbread (page 182) or Vanilla Bean Biscotti (page 189). — MIMI

2 cups (480 ml) water

2 cinnamon sticks

2 teaspoons raw honey

2 shots whiskey

1 medium lemon

~~~~~ SEA LEVEL ~~~~~

Follow the recipe as noted.

In a small saucepan over high heat, add the water and cinnamon sticks. In two mugs, add into each 1 teaspoon honey and 1 shot whiskey.

Slice the lemon into ½-inch slices. Once the water is boiling and has turned a pale tan color, remove from the heat. Pour the hot water into each mug and stir to combine completely.

Add a cinnamon stick into each mug. Add the lemon slices.

Elderberry Mojito

Makes 2 mojitos

Elderberries grow wild all over the Eastern Sierra in the fall; you can find and pick these tiny purple berries near climbing and hiking trails. They are a local mountain superfood that bursts with antioxidants and immune system–boosting properties. Naturally, I decided to make a cocktail with them. Maybe the best thing about this recipe is that the elderberry syrup can be used as an elixir. Store the extra syrup in your fridge and take a spoonful after a rough night. — MIMI

ELDERBERRY SYRUP

¼ cup (57 g) destemmed elderberries

¼ cup (57 g) cane sugar

¼ cup (60 ml) water

MOJITO

¼ cup fresh lemon juice (about 1 medium lemon)

1 tablespoon (14 g) cane sugar

4 fresh mint leaves, more for garnish

2 tablespoons plus 2 teaspoons Elderberry Syrup

2 shots Bacardi rum

12 ounces (355 ml) sparkling water

〰〰〰 SEA LEVEL 〰〰〰

Follow the recipe as noted.

To make the syrup: In a small saucepan, add the elderberries, ¼ cup cane sugar, and water. Put over medium heat and simmer until the mixture has reduced by about half (to about ¼ cup) and the syrup is thick; it will take about 10 to 15 minutes.

Remove from the heat and strain the syrup. Discard the mashed elderberries. Let the syrup chill in the fridge.

To make the mojito: In a small bowl, add the lemon juice and cane sugar. Stir to dissolve the cane sugar.

In two glasses, muddle 2 fresh mint leaves in each glass. Add 4 teaspoons of the elderberry syrup to each glass. Fill with ice. Add in 2 tablespoons of the lemon juice mixture and 1 shot of rum to each glass. Fill with sparkling water.

Top with fresh mint leaves and serve. Store extra Elderberry Syrup in fridge for up to 2 weeks.

Glühwein

Makes 4 to 6 servings

One trip in particular stands out vividly from the beginning of my snowboarding career. I was in my early twenties and traveling solo in Munich, Germany, right before Christmas. It was there at a Christmas market where I was first introduced to glühwein (which translates into English as "glow wine"). It was snowing like it does in the movies, and all I could smell was citrus, cinnamon, and wine. Not knowing too much about this customary holiday German drink, I bought some. The first sip transformed my taste buds: It was like Christmas in a cup. This drink takes your typical glass of red wine to a new level, and it's a sure way to impress your guests for the holidays. — KIMMY

2 medium oranges

1 medium lemon

1 bottle (750 ml) red wine

6 whole cloves

4 star anise pods

2 cinnamon sticks

1 vanilla bean

¼ cup (57 g) cane sugar

2 chai tea bags

SEA LEVEL

Follow the recipe as noted.

Using a vegetable peeler, peel the zest off one orange and the zest off the lemon in large strips. Juice one of the oranges and the lemon. Set juice aside.

Cut the other orange into ¼-inch-thick slices and save about half for glass garnishes. The remaining slices will be added to the red wine mixture.

Pour the red wine into a medium pot. Add the peels and the juice of the orange and lemon, the cloves, star anise, cinnamon sticks, and vanilla bean. Bring the mixture to a gentle simmer over medium heat. Add the cane sugar and stir until dissolved. Add the chai tea bags.

Allow the mixture to simmer for about 10 minutes; it will become fragrant. Ladle into mugs, leaving the spices in the pot. Garnish with an orange slice and serve. Keep the pot on a low simmer, so it's warm for refills.

Backyard Snow Cones

Makes 4 to 6 servings

Growing up, my crew was made up of my best friend and next door neighbor, Celeste, and our two brothers. The four of us pretty much did everything together. When it snowed a decent amount (which was rare in Chicago), we spent all our time outside. After we exhausted ourselves sledding, we searched out fresh snow to make snow cones. Our toppings were made up of maple syrup, chocolate sauce, or defrosted freeze pops—pretty much whatever we could find in the kitchen. If we had this syrup on hand, they would have been even better. — MIMI

BLUEBERRY

1 cup (170 grams) blueberries

1 cup (226 grams) cane sugar

1¼ cups (300 ml) water

STRAWBERRY

1 cup (170 grams)
  strawberries, destemmed

1 cup (226 grams) cane sugar

1¼ cups (300 ml) water

RASPBERRY

1 cup (142 grams) raspberries

1 cup (226 grams) cane sugar

1¼ cups (300 ml) water

∿∿∿ SEA LEVEL ∿∿∿

Follow the recipe as noted.

In a small saucepan, add the fruit, cane sugar, and 1 cup of the water. Put over medium heat, stirring frequently until sugar has completely dissolved. Increase the heat to high and boil for 1 to 2 minutes.

Decrease the heat to medium and simmer until the mixture has reduced by about half. Remove from the heat.

Add in the remaining ¼ cup of water and whisk to combine completely. Transfer to a squeeze bottle and store in the fridge until ready to use.

To serve, gather fresh snow in a cup and pour syrups over the top.

White Out Shake

Makes 2 shakes

I used to spend my summers working at a snowboard camp in Oregon. Almost every day, we'd stop at Dairy Queen on the way down from Mount Hood. DQ Blizzards became part of my summer routine, and since then, the only thing that's changed is my desire for higher-quality ingredients. I have made my own version here, adding in Vanilla Bean Biscotti (page 189). For an extra-special treat, top it with Whipped Cream (page 131). — MIMI

2 Vanilla Bean Biscotti (page 189)

16 ounces (454 g) vanilla bean ice cream

1 cup (240 ml) milk

2 tablespoons (30 ml) heavy whipping cream

1 tablespoon plus 1 teaspoon King Arthur Flour's Malted Milk Powder

Whipped Cream (page 131) for topping

〜〜〜 SEA LEVEL 〜〜〜

Follow the recipe as noted.

Chop the biscotti into small pieces. Set aside.

In a blender, add the vanilla bean ice cream, milk, whipping cream, and malted milk powder. Blend until smooth. Add three-quarters of the chopped biscotti into the blender and stir with a spatula to combine.

Transfer the shake into two cups and top with the remaining biscotti pieces. Top with Whipped Cream.

HEARTY EATS

W*hile most people would immedi*ately define hearty meals as being large, big portioned, or dense with meat, I think of the word *hearty* as a way food can make me feel: full, satisfied, and well nourished. The recipes in this chapter are designed from the heart, and they will nourish your body with high-quality ingredients and make you feel good any time you enjoy them.

I love indulging in a large bowl of my Hearty Winter Stew (page 157). This recipe has filled me up after many long, snowy days in the backcountry. One time in particular, I left for my day on the mountains with a batch cooking on low in my slow cooker. I had planned it so when I got home from filming in the back country, it would be ready. Like any outdoor enthusiast knows, time has a tendency to get away from you, and instead of getting back at 5 p.m., I got home around 9 p.m. that night. We had experienced a snowmobile breakdown about 20 miles from the trailhead, just as the sun was setting. We had to throw on our headlamps, rig up a tow system with tie downs, and pull the snow-mobile out of the mountains with our other machine. When I finally got to my truck, I was hungry, tired, and just wanted to curl up in my bed. But as soon as I got home and opened my door, the incredible smell of the stew wafted toward me. I quickly remembered that a hearty dinner was already there and waiting for me—and it couldn't have come at a better time. I needed more than just food after that crazy day, but coming home to dinner already prepared was a present in and of itself. All I had to do was ladle it into a bowl and relax into the couch.

All the recipes in this chapter will fill your heart as well as your belly. Whether you share them with friends or family, the unique preparations and presentations have a tendency to impress whoever you make them for. Some of them are jam-packed with vegetables, and some include meats. If you're looking to feed more people or get more protein, you can always add meat to veggie recipes like Baked Mac 'N' Cheese (page 158) or Harvest Chili (page 165). We hope this chapter gives you new and heartfelt cooking adventures.

—KIMMY

Bagel Sandwich

Makes 1 sandwich

I love bagel sandwiches because you can eat them for breakfast, brunch,
lunch, or dinner. And I love eating breakfast for dinner. When I'm starving
after a long day, I want to make a fast but equally satisfying meal, and a bagel
sandwich checks all the boxes. —MIMI

1 Spicy Everything Bagel
  (page 35)

1 tablespoon (14 g) salted butter

1 large egg

2 tablespoons cream cheese

2 slices bacon, cooked to your liking

¼ avocado, sliced

〜〜〜 SEA LEVEL 〜〜〜

Follow the recipe as noted.

Slice the bagel in half and toast to your liking.

In a small frying pan, add the butter. Put over medium heat and
once the butter has melted, place a 3½-inch cookie cutter into the
pan. Crack the egg into the cookie cutter; this will help it from
spreading out so it is the size of the bagel. When the egg starts to
cook, remove the cutter and flip the egg until it's cooked on both
sides. Remove from the heat.

Spread the cream cheese onto each side of bagel. On one side place
the bacon pieces, then add the egg and avocado slices. Top with
the other half of the bagel.

Crag Club Sandwich

Makes 2 sandwiches

There's nothing like the hunger you get while rock climbing. So when you can open your pack in the middle of a long day at the crag to find a ready-made sandwich like this, there truly is nothing better. (Except maybe having a cookie for dessert.) — KIMMY

4 slices Mountain Bread (page 33)

2 tablespoons mayonnaise

4 slices sharp Cheddar cheese

4 slices applewood smoked bacon, cooked to your liking

4 slices oven-roasted turkey

½ medium avocado, sliced

Pinch of Everything Spice Mix (page 29)

1 medium tomato, sliced

½ cup (15 g) butter lettuce

～～～ SEA LEVEL ～～～

Follow the recipe as noted.

On two slices of bread, spread 1 tablespoon of mayonnaise on each. Lay cheese slices on top of the mayonnaise, then the bacon slices, and then the turkey slices.

On the other two slices of bread, arrange the avocado slices and sprinkle each slice with Everything Spice Mix. Lay the tomato slices on top, and then the lettuce.

Put the two topped pieces of bread together to make two sandwiches, and cut each sandwich in half.

Pizza Bread

Makes 4 slices

Individual mini pizzas have a special place in my heart. These are a grown-up
version of the ones I made as a kid, and they are a quick and easy dinner to prepare
after a long day. If you have Mountain Bread (page 33) on hand, you'll have
dinner ready in no time. — MIMI

2 tablespoons (28 grams)
salted butter, softened

1 garlic clove, minced

4 slices Mountain Bread (page 33)

2 medium tomatoes

12 slices (6 ounces; 170 g)
mozzarella

Fresh basil leaves for garnish

Parmesan for garnish

Crushed red peppers for
garnish (optional)

〰〰〰 SEA LEVEL 〰〰〰

Bake at 450°F for 12 to 14 minutes,
or until the cheese is melted.

Preheat the oven to 450°F.

In a small saucepan, add the butter and garlic. Cook over medium
heat for 1 to 2 minutes, until the garlic starts to brown and is
fragrant.

Using a pastry brush, spread the garlic butter onto each slice of
bread. Slice the tomatoes into ¼-inch slices. Add about three
slices of the tomato onto each slice of bread. Add three slices of the
mozzarella on top of the tomatoes and bake for 10 to 12 minutes,
or until the cheese is melted.

Top with fresh basil, Parmesan, and/or crushed red peppers
(optional).

Personal Cauliflower Pizzas

Makes 2 pizzas

As a fun reward for doing chores when I was little, my mom and I would go out for pizza two times a month. I gave up that tradition long ago. Instead, I make my own delicious and creative pizzas when I'm in the mood for them. Because of the perfect blend of vegetables, cheese, and herbs, these taste just like my old favorites, but are much healthier! —KIMMY

CRUST

1 large head cauliflower

1 large egg

¼ teaspoon basil

¼ teaspoon parsley

¼ teaspoon oregano

¼ teaspoon garlic powder

¼ teaspoon fine sea salt

2 tablespoons (14 g) grated mozzarella

⅓ cup (85 g) packed crumbled goat cheese

TOPPINGS

¼ cup (63 g) tomato sauce

¾ cup (85 g) grated mozzarella

2 small tomatoes, sliced

¼ small red onion, sliced

½ small red pepper, diced

¾ cup (85 g) shredded chicken

4 sprigs fresh cilantro

∿∿∿ SEA LEVEL ∿∿∿

Bake the cauliflower at 400°F for 45 to 50 minutes, or until golden brown, stirring occasionally. Bake the formed cauliflower crusts for 25 minutes, or until golden brown. Bake the topped pizzas for 10 to 14 minutes, or until cheese is bubbly and golden brown.

Preheat the oven to 400°F. Line a baking sheet with parchment paper.

To make the crusts: Cut the cauliflower into florets. Using a food processor with the grater attachment, grate the florets into a consistency similar to rice. Grate enough cauliflower to produce three packed-full cups of cauliflower rice.

Place the cauliflower rice evenly on the prepared baking sheet. Bake for 28 to 32 minutes, until golden brown, stirring occasionally. You'll notice the cauliflower rice will shrink significantly. Once the rice is golden brown, remove from the oven and place the cauliflower on a clean dish towel. Squeeze the rice to remove excess moisture.

Place the rice into a large mixing bowl. Add the egg, basil, parsley, oregano, garlic powder, sea salt, mozzarella, and goat cheese. Mix thoroughly with a wooden spoon.

Line a baking sheet with parchment paper. Form the rice mixture into two small 4-inch disks. As you form the disks try to keep them ⅓-inch thick.

Bake for 25 minutes, or until firm and golden brown. Remove from oven and add the toppings. Top each pizza with 2 table-spoons tomato sauce, then grated mozzarella, tomato slices, red onion, red pepper, and chicken.

Bake the topped pizzas for 8 to 12 minutes, or until the cheese is bubbly and golden brown. Garnish each pizza with 2 sprigs of cilantro.

Hearty Winter Stew

Make 6 servings

I have fond memories of coming home from snowboarding to a house filled with the aromas of my mom's delicious beef stew brewing in the slow cooker. She would load up my bowl with chunky tender meat and vegetables, and then pair it with a piece of buttered Mountain Bread (page 33). It was such a filling and comforting meal. — KIMMY

2 pounds (907 g) grass-fed beef chuck

3 teaspoons fine sea salt, more if needed

3 tablespoons (45 ml) olive oil

½ medium red onion, diced

2 tablespoons (16 g) all-purpose flour

2 medium tomatoes, chopped

2 tablespoons (28 g) tomato paste

5 garlic cloves, peeled and coarsely chopped

2 cups (480 ml) red wine (I use Syrah)

1 teaspoon black pepper, more if needed

2 cups (480 ml) beef or chicken broth

2 bay leaves

4 sprigs fresh rosemary

¼ cup (5 g) chopped fresh sage

1 tablespoon (2 g) parsley

3 large carrots, peeled and sliced into chunks

8 ounces (226 g) mushrooms, sliced

8 to 10 baby gold potatoes, halved

2 stalks celery chopped

1 medium fennel bulb, sliced into ½-inch wedges

Mountain Bread (page 33) to serve

Heat the slow cooker on low before adding the ingredients. Cut the beef into 2- to 3-inch pieces and trim any excess fat as you cut it. Place the beef in a medium bowl and season it with 2 teaspoons of the sea salt.

In a large skillet, heat the olive oil over medium heat. In two or three batches quickly sear the beef until browned on each side, for 1 to 2 minutes. Remove and set aside in a clean mixing bowl.

Add the onion to the same skillet and cook until translucent, 2 to 3 minutes. Sprinkle the all-purpose flour over the seared beef until it's all lightly coated. Add the beef back to the skillet with the onions. Stir in the tomatoes, tomato paste, garlic, ½ cup of the red wine, 1 teaspoon of the sea salt, and pepper. Bring to a simmer for 3 minutes.

In the slow cooker, add the broth, the remaining 1½ cups red wine, bay leaves, rosemary, sage, and parsley. Stir thoroughly, and then add the carrots, mushrooms, potatoes, celery, and fennel to the slow cooker. Mix the ingredients together.

Slowly pour the beef mixture into the slow cooker and stir to combine all the ingredients. The liquid should cover the beef, add more broth if needed. Cook on low for 6 to 8 hours or on high for 3 to 4 hours.

Season to taste with more salt or pepper. Serve with Mountain Bread.

Store in an airtight container in the fridge for up to 5 days.

·········· GLUTEN-FREE ··········

Replace the all-purpose flour with 2 tablespoons (19 g) gluten-free flour blend.

〜〜〜 SEA LEVEL 〜〜〜

Follow the recipe as noted.

Baked Mac 'N' Cheese

Makes 8 servings

Macaroni and cheese was the first meal I learned to make on my own. Even though it was just from a box, I felt like I was creating my own version by putting in less butter and more milk. I have been making macaroni and cheese ever since, but I have graduated to truly making my own. I love preparing this recipe, because it makes a large portion that is just as good reheated as it is the day you make it. My husband, Delaney, and I will have it for days. If you want some extra protein, add sliced ham, turkey, or chicken. — MIMI

4 quarts (3.8 L) water

1 pound (454 g) elbow noodles

1 teaspoon fine sea salt

3 cups (6 ounces; 170 g) chopped broccoli

8 ounces (226 g) mushrooms, thinly sliced

¼ cup plus 2 tablespoons (85 g) salted butter

3 cups (270 g) grated white Cheddar cheese

1½ cups (170 g) grated mozzarella cheese

½ cup (113 g) sour cream

1 cup (240 ml) milk

1 tablespoon Everything Spice Mix (page 29)

·············· GLUTEN-FREE ··············

Use gluten-free noodles.

〜〜〜 SEA LEVEL 〜〜〜

Bake at 375°F for 25 to 30 minutes, or until the cheese is lightly browned.

In an 8-quart pot, boil the 4 quarts water. Once boiling, add the noodles and sea salt. Cook the noodles until done, for 8 to 10 minutes or for the time specified on the package. Strain the noodles and transfer back to the pot.

While the noodles are cooking, steam the broccoli by adding about an inch of water into a small saucepan. Place a steamer basket in the saucepan, add the broccoli, and cover with a lid. Let steam for about 5 minutes or until the broccoli is tender and bright in color. Set aside.

Sauté the mushrooms by adding the 2 tablespoons butter and mushrooms to a medium frying pan. Cook over medium heat until the mushrooms shrink and brown. Remove from the heat, set aside.

Preheat the oven to 375°F. Add the Cheddar cheese, ½ cup of the mozzarella cheese, sour cream, ¼ cup butter, and milk to the hot noodles. Stir to combine completely. Add the broccoli, mushrooms, and Everything Spice Mix and stir to combine completely.

Transfer the noodle mixture to a 9-by-13-inch baking pan and spread evenly. Top with the remaining 1 cup mozzarella cheese. Bake for 15 to 20 minutes, or until the cheese is lightly browned.

Store in an airtight container in the fridge for up to 5 days.

Tamari Orange Chicken

Makes 4 servings

Because I'm an athlete, eating clean and healthy food has always been a big focus for me. Organic chicken, specifically, has been my way of adding lean protein to my diet. Combining it with fresh stir-fried veggies and brown rice provides a well-balanced, delicious meal that's complete and satisfying. This recipe is on heavy rotation at my house. It is really adaptable, too, because you can switch up the vegetables to whatever you have in the fridge. If you don't need this dish to be gluten-free, you can use regular soy sauce instead of tamari. — **KIMMY**

CHICKEN

1 large orange

2 tablespoons (30 ml) olive oil

1½ pounds (680 g) chicken breast

1 tablespoon Everything Spice Mix (page 29)

½ cup (120 ml) tamari soy sauce

¼ cup (85 g) raw honey

VEGGIES

2 tablespoons (30 ml) olive oil

2 teaspoons fresh diced ginger

2 teaspoons fresh diced turmeric

3 garlic cloves, diced

1 small red onion, diced

8 ounces (226 g) mushrooms, sliced

½ teaspoon fine sea salt

1 medium red pepper, sliced

1 bunch asparagus, ends removed

2 cups (113 g) chopped broccoli florets, destemmed

RICE

2 cups cooked brown rice for serving

To make the chicken: Cut the orange in half and juice each half, to get ¼ cup (60 ml) fresh orange juice. Set the juice aside. Peel the orange halves and set the peels aside.

Heat the 2 tablespoons olive oil in a medium frying pan, add the chicken breast, and season each side with Everything Spice Mix.

In a small bowl, mix the tamari, honey, and orange juice. Pour ¼ cup of the tamari mixture over the chicken in the frying pan. Set aside the remaining tamari mixture. Cover the chicken with a lid and let simmer on low heat for 20 to 25 minutes, flipping if necessary, until fully cooked. Remove the chicken and slice into pieces.

To make the veggies: Heat the 2 tablespoons olive oil in a large skillet. Add the ginger, turmeric, and garlic and allow to become fragrant, 2 to 3 minutes. Add the red onion, and cook until translucent, about 1 to 2 minutes.

Add the mushrooms, orange peels, and sea salt and simmer for 3 to 5 minutes. Add the red pepper, asparagus, broccoli, and the remaining ¾ cup tamari mixture. Simmer and let steam with lid partially cracked for 10 minutes.

Serve the chicken and veggies with the brown rice.

Store in an airtight container in the fridge for up to 5 days.

〜〜〜〜 SEA LEVEL 〜〜〜〜

Follow the recipe as noted.

Bison Wild Rice

Makes 4 servings

Bison is my top pick for red meat because it's more environmentally sustainable than beef and is also loaded with lean protein. This unique and hearty rice dish can be served by itself or as a side to a main course for a hungry house of guests. —KIMMY

BISON

1 tablespoon (15 ml) olive oil

1 pound (454 g) ground bison

½ cup (60 g) diced yellow onion

2 cloves garlic, minced

1 tablespoon (22 g) Dijon mustard

1 teaspoon cumin

1 teaspoon parsley

½ teaspoon fine sea salt

¼ teaspoon black pepper

MUSHROOMS

2 tablespoons (30 ml) olive oil

8 ounces (227 g) mushrooms, chopped

½ teaspoon garlic powder

½ teaspoon fine sea salt

¼ teaspoon cayenne pepper

1½ packed cups (55 g) destemmed and chopped kale leaves

¼ cup (60 ml) white wine

RICE

3 cups cooked wild rice (made with chicken stock instead of water)

SEA LEVEL

Follow the recipe as noted.

To make the bison: In a 10-inch cast iron skillet, heat the 1 tablespoon olive oil on medium heat. Add the bison, onion, and garlic. With a wooden spoon, break the bison into pieces. Stir in the mustard, cumin, parsley, ½ teaspoon sea salt, and pepper. Continue to cook until the bison is brown and cooked to your liking. Remove from the heat.

To make the mushrooms: In a medium saucepan, heat the 2 tablespoons olive oil. Add the mushrooms, garlic powder, ½ teaspoon sea salt, and cayenne and sauté 2 to 3 minutes. Add the kale and wine to the mushrooms and simmer covered on low heat for 5 to 10 minutes. Remove from the heat and add to the bison mixture in the skillet.

Fold the rice into the bison skillet mixture.

Store in an airtight container in the fridge for up to 5 days.

Harvest Chili

Makes 8 servings

If you are expecting a houseful of guests and don't want to spend all day cooking a lavish meal, let this chili be your answer. The flavor of this hearty chili will satisfy even the most carnivorous eaters, even though it's vegan! My favorite way to serve this is with a side of Sweet Potato Fries (page 123). — **KIMMY**

One 28-ounce can diced tomatoes

2¾ cups (660 ml) vegetable broth

Two 15-ounce cans (850 g) black beans, drained and rinsed

Two 15-ounce cans (850 g) pinto beans, drained and rinsed

1 medium sweet potato, peeled and chopped

One 6-ounce can (170 g) tomato paste

2 tablespoons (28 g) coconut oil

1 medium yellow onion, diced

¾ cup (80 g) chopped fresh fennel

6 garlic cloves, diced

2 tablespoons (10 g) cumin

2 tablespoons (14 g) chili powder

1 teaspoon coriander

¼ teaspoon cayenne pepper

1 pound (454 g) mushrooms, chopped

¼ cup (60 ml) brewed espresso or black coffee

2 tablespoons (30 ml) water

½ teaspoon fine sea salt

¼ teaspoon black pepper

1 medium avocado, chopped for serving

Fresh cilantro for serving

Nutritional yeast for serving

Preheat a slow cooker to a high temperature setting. Add the tomatoes, vegetable broth, black beans, pinto beans, sweet potato, and tomato paste.

In a large saucepan, heat the coconut oil over medium. Add the onion, fennel, garlic, cumin, chili powder, coriander, and cayenne pepper. Sauté for 3 to 5 minutes, or until caramelized. Add the mushrooms to the saucepan and stir in the espresso and water. Simmer with the lid on for 5 to 10 minutes, or until tender. Remove from the heat and add to the slow cooker along with the sea salt and pepper.

Cook on high for 3 to 4 hours. Serve with the avocado, cilantro, and a sprinkle of nutritional yeast on top.

Store in an airtight container in the fridge for up to 5 days.

~~~~ SEA LEVEL ~~~~

Follow the recipe as noted.

Pesto Zucchini Lasagna

Makes 6 servings

This recipe is designed to make you think outside the box, literally. Instead of a box of pasta noodles, this lasagna is made with strips of zucchini. It's a mouth-watering spin on lasagna that is packed full of veggies. It's even fun to make. You can add meat to this dish for more protein: I most commonly add precooked chopped up chicken breast. **—KIMMY**

PESTO CASHEW CHEESE

1 cup (142 g) raw unsalted cashews

½ cup (120 ml) unsweetened almond milk

¼ cup (5 g) packed fresh basil leaves

3 garlic cloves

2 tablespoons (30 ml) fresh lemon juice

2 tablespoons (14 g) nutritional yeast

½ teaspoon fine sea salt

TOMATO SAUCE

2 tablespoons (30 ml) olive oil

1 medium red onion, diced

8 ounces (226 g) mushrooms, sliced

3 garlic cloves, minced

½ teaspoon fine sea salt

¼ teaspoon garlic powder

¼ teaspoon oregano

¼ teaspoon thyme

One 14.5-ounce can (411 g) diced tomatoes

One 14-ounce can (397 g) artichoke hearts, liquid drained and chopped

One 6-ounce can (170 g) tomato paste

¼ cup (5 g) packed chopped fresh basil leaves

2 teaspoons Everything Spice Mix (page 29)

¼ cup water

To make the cashew cheese: Soak the cashews in a bowl of cool water for 20 to 30 minutes, or until tender. Drain and rinse the cashews. Place them in a food processor with the almond milk, basil, garlic, lemon juice, nutritional yeast, and ½ teaspoon sea salt. Blend for 30 seconds. Scrape down the sides and bottom of processor, and blend again for 30 seconds or until smooth. Set aside.

To make the tomato sauce: On medium heat, add the olive oil to a frying pan. Add the red onion and mushrooms, and sauté until the onion is translucent, for 1 to 3 minutes. Stir in the garlic, ½ teaspoon sea salt, garlic powder, oregano, and thyme and sauté for 1 more minute.

Add the tomatoes, artichoke hearts, tomato paste, basil, and Everything Spice Mix. Add the water to thin the sauce. Simmer for 5 to 10 minutes. Remove from the heat and set aside.

(continued)

1½ pounds (680 g) zucchini

1 tablespoon fine sea salt

4 cups (168 g) baby spinach

Fresh basil for garnish

～～～ SEA LEVEL ～～～

Bake, covered, for 40 minutes. Remove
cover and bake for 20 to 25 minutes,
or until the top is golden brown.

To make the zucchini noodles: Using a mandoline, slice each zucchini longways into ¼-inch slices.

Lay the zucchini noodles evenly spaced on a clean surface (I prefer to use baking sheets for ease). Lightly sprinkle 1 tablespoon sea salt over the sliced noodles to pull the moisture out of the zucchini. Let sit for 15 minutes, or until droplets of water are abundant on the tops of zucchinis.

Using clean dish towels, pat zucchinis dry and layer them on clean, dry dishtowels to absorb excess moisture.

To make the lasagna: Preheat the oven to 375°F. Lightly grease a 9-by-13-inch baking dish. Thinly spread 1 cup of the tomato sauce on the bottom of the baking dish.

Layer 10 to 12 zucchini slices side by side (slightly overlapped) across the bottom of the dish on top of the tomato sauce. Layer another 1 cup of tomato sauce and ½ cup of the cashew cheese. Gently spread the two sauces across the zucchini slices with a spatula. Layer 2 cups of the baby spinach evenly on top. Repeat this process again for the second layer. Top with the remaining zucchini slices, tomato sauce, and cashew cheese.

Bake, covered, for 30 minutes. Remove cover and bake for 15 to 20 minutes, or until the top is golden brown. Allow the lasagna to cool for 15 minutes before cutting and serving. Add fresh basil for garnish.

Store in an airtight container in the fridge for up to 3 days.

COOKIES & BARS

Cookies inspired my love of baking simply because I wanted to eat them. As a child I waited all year for Christmas, Greek Easter, or Thanksgiving to arrive because those were the holidays when my YiaYia ("Grandma" in Greek) baked her famous Koloodia Cookies (page 186). So when I started baking on my own, cookies were the first thing I conquered, thanks to the recipe on the back of the bag of Nestlé semi-sweet chocolate chips. Having only one cookie recipe got old after a while, however. And because this was way before Pinterest and Instagram, if you wanted inspiration you had to find it yourself. So that's what I did.

By the time we opened Dessert'D, I had tons of cookie recipes. They came from years of experimenting on my own and asking my friends what flavors they'd like to see in a cookie. When we opened our doors, cookies were the only thing on our menu! Looking back, it's a little hard to believe, considering that we bake so many other desserts now. But during that first year, all we sold were

cookies. We even got a little bit of a hard time about it from some people in town. Why did we only sell cookies? How were we going to "make it" by only selling cookies? While the skeptical people were busy judging us, everyone else was busy trying our cookies. Turns out, people loved them just as much as we did!

Before being known for Dessert'D Organic Bake Shop, I was simply known as the girl with the cookies. I baked them in my free time and brought them everywhere I went—which was mostly work, friend's houses, and snowboarding. I'd see my friends on the deck at the mountain and they'd ask me if I had any cookies. I'd usually pull them out of my pocket and hand them over. Two months before moving back to Mammoth Lakes, California, and opening Dessert'D, I saw Kimmy at the mountain and I handed her a cookie in the parking lot. Even after all these years, I believe I am still saved in Kimmy's e-mail contacts as Mimi Cookies. —MIMI

Dark Chocolate Chunk Cookies

Makes 24 cookies

After a long day in the mountains, I get really hungry. And I also feel like I deserve a treat. That's why I love these cookies, which are actually Paleo friendly. These amazing, hearty cookies have dark chocolate that hits my cravings for sweets. And because they're made with almond flour, they have some added protein that really satisfies. The result is the perfect snack in between an adventure and après. — MIMI

½ cup (113 g) coconut oil

Scant 1⅔ cups (226 g) coconut sugar

½ teaspoon ground vanilla bean

2 cups (198 g) almond flour

½ cup plus 1 tablespoon (57 g) coconut flour

1½ teaspoons baking powder

½ teaspoon fine sea salt

2 large eggs

¾ cup (106 g) dark chocolate chunks

~~~~~~~ SEA LEVEL ~~~~~~~

Bake at 375°F for 11 minutes, or until the cookies look puffy and set.

Preheat the oven to 375°F. Line two baking sheets with parchment paper.

In the bowl of a stand mixer fitted with the paddle attachment, add the coconut oil, coconut sugar, and ground vanilla bean. Mix on low until all the ingredients are combined and no chunks of coconut oil remain.

In a separate bowl, add the almond flour, coconut flour, baking powder, and sea salt and whisk together. Add the eggs to the coconut oil mixture and add the flour mixture right on top. Mix on low until almost combined; you'll still see chunks of flour. Add the dark chocolate chunks and mix on low until combined.

Using your hands, form the cookie dough into 24 balls and place them on the prepared baking sheets. Twelve will fit on each sheet. Flatten them slightly so they look like disks that are about 2¼ inches in diameter.

Bake for 8 minutes, or until the cookies look puffy and set. Let cool completely on the baking sheets.

Store in an airtight container for up to 7 days.

Peanut Butter Dark Chocolate Chunk Cookies

Makes 20 cookies

When we were opening Dessert'D, Kimmy wanted me to add vegan cookies
to our menu. I went through what seemed like hundreds of recipes before
I finally created this one. This was the first vegan cookie we put on the
menu, and it's still one of our favorites today. The best part? Your friends
won't even be able to tell it's vegan! —MIMI

½ cup (113 g) Earth Balance
coconut spread

½ cup (113 g) cane sugar,
plus extra for topping

½ cup (113 g) packed
dark brown sugar

1¼ teaspoons vanilla extract

¾ cup plus 1 tablespoon
(226 g) peanut butter

2 tablespoons plus 1 teaspoon
(35 ml) unsweetened
vanilla coconut milk

1¼ cups plus 2 tablespoons
(177 g) all-purpose flour

½ teaspoon baking soda

½ teaspoon fine sea salt

1 cup (142 g) dark chocolate
chunks

Preheat the oven to 375°F. Line two baking sheets with
parchment paper.

In the bowl of a stand mixer fitted with the paddle attachment,
add the coconut spread, cane sugar, brown sugar, and vanilla
extract. Mix on low until combined and no chunks of coconut
spread remain. Add the peanut butter and coconut milk and mix
for three to four rotations; do not overmix.

In a separate bowl, add the flour, baking soda, and sea salt and
whisk together. Add to the sugar mixture and mix on low until a
dough forms. Add the dark chocolate chunks and mix on low until
combined.

Using your hands, or a 1¾-inch cookie scoop, form the dough into
20 balls and place on the prepared baking sheets. Flatten each ball
slightly so they are about 2 inches in diameter.

Bake for 8 minutes, or until cracked and set on top. Sprinkle with
cane sugar immediately after they come out of the oven. Let cool
completely on the baking sheets.

Store in an airtight container for up to 7 days.

.... GLUTEN-FREE ....

Replace the all-purpose flour with
1 cup plus 2 tablespoons (177 g) gluten-
free flour blend.

~~~~~ SEA LEVEL ~~~~~

Bake at 375°F for 11 minutes, or until
cracked and set on top.

Brown Butter Oatmeal Raisin Cookies

Makes 18 cookies

Browning the butter takes these classic oatmeal raisin cookies to the next
level. Brown butter is something that gives extra flavor and allure to these
cookies, and it will leave your friends wondering what makes these "standard"
oatmeal raisin cookies so good! — MIMI

½ cup (113 g) salted butter

½ cup (113 g) packed
  dark brown sugar

¼ cup (57 g) cane sugar

1 teaspoon vanilla extract

2 large eggs

1¼ cups (160 g) all-purpose flour

1 cup plus 2 tablespoons
  (113 g) rolled oats

½ teaspoon baking soda

½ teaspoon fine sea salt

¾ cup (117 g) raisins

.... GLUTEN-FREE ....

Use gluten-free oats. Replace the
all-purpose flour with 1 cup plus
1½ tablespoons (174 g) gluten-free
flour blend.

〜〜〜 SEA LEVEL 〜〜〜

Bake at 375°F for 11 minutes, or until the
cookies look lightly puffed and set.

Add the butter to a small saucepan and put over medium heat.
Allow the butter to melt, stirring occasionally. Once the butter
has completely melted, it will start to brown. It may bubble up
and turn white, which will make it hard to see the color. If this
happens, remove from the heat until the bubbles calm down, and
then return to heat if it's not done. When it's done the butter will
be a light brown color, similar to maple syrup. The milk solids will
also sink to the bottom and form small darker specs. This can take
5 to 10 minutes; be sure to remove the butter from the heat as soon
as it has browned, as it can burn quickly. Allow to cool completely
before beginning next step.

Preheat the oven to 375°F. Line two baking sheets with
parchment paper.

In the bowl of a stand mixer fitted with the paddle attachment,
add the brown butter, brown sugar, cane sugar, and vanilla
extract. Mix on low until combined and it looks like a dark paste.
Add the eggs and mix just slightly, enough to break the yolks.

In a separate bowl, add the flour, oats, baking soda, and sea salt
and whisk together. Add into the butter mixture with the raisins
and mix on low until combined into a dough.

Using your hands, or a 1¾-inch cookie scoop, form dough into
18 balls and place on the prepared baking sheets. Flatten each ball
slightly so they are about 2 inches in diameter.

Bake for 8 minutes, or until the cookies look lightly puffed and set.
Let cool completely on the baking sheets.

Store in an airtight container for up to 7 days.

Iced Apple Cinnamon Cookies

Makes 18 cookies

When we first opened Dessert'D, Mimi had cookies on the menu named after our "ambassadors." These ambassadors were mostly snowboarders who were our friends. Since I was one of them, I got my own cookie. Mimi created it for me based on what I told her I wanted to see in a cookie. This cookie is still one of my favorites today! —KIMMY

DOUGH

½ cup (113 g) salted butter, softened

¾ cup (170 g) cane sugar

1 teaspoon vanilla extract

2 large eggs

2 cups (383 g) pastry flour

2 teaspoons cinnamon

1¼ teaspoons baking powder

½ teaspoon fine sea salt

1 medium apple (such as Gala, Fuji, or Cripps Pink), chopped into cubes

ICING

Heaping 2⅓ cups (340 g) powdered sugar, sifted

¼ cup plus 1 tablespoon heavy whipping cream

¼ cup (57 g) salted butter, softened

1 teaspoon vanilla extract

TOPPING

1 tablespoon (14 g) cane sugar

¼ teaspoon cinnamon

·············· GLUTEN-FREE ··············

Replace the pastry flour with 2½ cups plus 1 tablespoon (397 g) gluten-free flour blend.

〰〰〰 SEA LEVEL 〰〰〰

Bake at 375°F for 11 minutes, or until the cookies look set.

Preheat the oven to 375°F. Line two baking sheets with parchment paper.

To make the dough: In the bowl of a stand mixer fitted with the paddle attachment, add the ½ cup butter, ¾ cup cane sugar, and 1 teaspoon vanilla extract. Mix on low until combined and no chunks of butter remain. Add the eggs and mix just slightly, enough to break the yolks.

In a separate bowl, add the pastry flour, 2 teaspoons cinnamon, baking powder, and sea salt and whisk together. Add to the butter mixture and mix on low until combined into a dough. Add the apple chunks and fold in to combine completely so you don't break the apples.

Using your hands, or a 1¾-inch cookie scoop, form the dough into 18 balls and place on the prepared baking sheets. Flatten each ball slightly so they are about 2¼ inches in diameter. Bake for 8 minutes or until the cookies look set. Let cool completely on the baking sheets.

To make the icing: In the bowl of a stand mixer fitted with the paddle attachment, add all the icing ingredients. Mix on low until combined, then speed up the mixer to high. Scrape down the sides of the bowl and mix again for 1 minute or until light and fluffy. Using a piping bag or spatula, frost the cookies.

To make the topping: In a small dish, mix together the 1 tablespoon cane sugar and ¼ teaspoon cinnamon. Sprinkle the cinnamon and sugar mixture on top of the frosted cookies.

Store in an airtight container for up to 3 days.

Bacon Chocolate Chip Cookie Skillet

Makes one 10-inch cookie skillet

There's nothing like a big, warm, gooey chocolate chip cookie straight from the oven. I've added bacon and sea salt to make this one sweet and salty. Serve it with a few scoops of vanilla bean ice cream for a real treat. — MIMI

DOUGH

½ cup (113 g) salted butter, softened

¼ cup plus 2 tablespoons (85 grams) cane sugar

¼ cup plus 2 tablespoons (85 grams) packed dark brown sugar

1 teaspoon vanilla extract

2 large eggs

2 cups (255 g) all-purpose flour

½ teaspoon baking soda

½ teaspoon fine sea salt

¾ cup (142 g) semi-sweet chocolate chips

6 slices applewood smoked bacon, cooked to your liking, chopped

TOPPING

1 teaspoon cane sugar

1 teaspoon fine sea salt

.... GLUTEN-FREE ....

Replace the all-purpose flour with 1¾ cups (269 g) gluten-free flour blend.

〰〰 SEA LEVEL 〰〰

Follow the recipe as noted.

Preheat the oven to 300°F.

To make the dough: In the bowl of a stand mixer fitted with the paddle attachment, add the butter, ¼ cup plus 2 tablespoons cane sugar, brown sugar, and vanilla extract. Mix on low until combined and no chunks of butter remain. Add the eggs and mix just slightly.

In a separate bowl, add the flour, baking soda, and ½ teaspoon sea salt and whisk together. Add to the butter mixture and mix on low until a stiff dough forms. Add the chocolate chips and bacon and mix until combined.

Press the dough into a 10-inch cast-iron skillet. Bake for 40 minutes, or until the cookie looks set in the middle.

To make the topping: In a small dish, add the 1 teaspoon cane sugar and 1 teaspoon sea salt and mix together. Sprinkle the mixture on top of the cookie immediately after coming out of the oven.

Serve immediately or store in an airtight container for up to 7 days.

Cranberry Orange Ginger Shortbread

Makes 16 cookies

These are not your store-bought, slice-and-bake cookies. The process, however,
is similar in that you make the dough ahead of time and stick it in the fridge.
When the dough is ready, all you have to do is slice and bake. This makes it
really easy to have fresh cookies, plus you can spend your day adventuring
instead of prepping. — MIMI

½ cup (113 g) salted butter,
softened

½ cup (71 g) powdered sugar, sifted

2 teaspoons orange flavor (such as
Frontier Co-op Orange Flavor)

½ teaspoon vanilla extract

1½ cups (191 g) all-purpose
flour

¼ teaspoon ginger

⅓ cup (43 g) dried cranberries

Cane sugar for dusting

〜〜〜 SEA LEVEL 〜〜〜

Bake at 350°F for 13 minutes, or until the
edges are golden brown.

In the bowl of a stand mixer fitted with the paddle attachment,
add the butter, powdered sugar, orange flavor, and vanilla extract.
Mix on low until you no longer see the powdered sugar; you will
still see chunks of butter at this stage and that is fine. Do not
overmix.

Add the flour, ginger, and cranberries to the butter mixture and
mix on low. This will seem like it's not coming together, but mix
until it almost does and looks like wet sand.

Transfer the dough to a piece of plastic wrap and shape it into
a log. The more you shape it, the more it should start to come
together. The log should be a rectangle that is about 6-by-2-
by-2 inches. Wrap it completely in plastic wrap. You can shape it
more and a little better once it's completely wrapped. Make the
sides smooth by forming it after it's wrapped. Place the cookie
dough in the fridge overnight.

Preheat the oven to 350°F. Line a baking sheet with parchment
paper. Unwrap the dough and trim off the edges. Slice the dough
log into 16 cookies that are about ¼-inch thick. Place on the
prepared baking sheet about ½-inch apart.

Bake for 12 minutes or until the edges are golden brown. Sprinkle
with cane sugar after coming out of the oven. Let cool completely
on the baking sheets.

Store in an airtight container for up to 7 days.

Spiced Spritz Cookies

Makes 50 cookies

These little holiday cookies are all you need for those times when you want to curl up in front a fire and watch Christmas movies. Add a Hot Toddy (page 136) and it just gets better. —MIMI

1 cup (226 g) salted butter, softened

¾ cup (170 g) cane sugar,
  plus extra for topping

2 teaspoons vanilla extract

1 large egg

2 cups (255 g) all-purpose flour

½ teaspoon cinnamon

½ teaspoon ginger

½ teaspoon cloves

·············· GLUTEN-FREE ··············

Replace the all-purpose flour with
1½ scant cups (227 g) gluten-free flour
blend and ½ cup plus 1 tablespoon (57 g)
coconut flour.

〰〰〰 SEA LEVEL 〰〰〰

Bake at 350°F for 13 minutes, or until
golden brown around the edges.

Preheat the oven to 350°F. Line two baking sheets with parchment paper.

In the bowl of a stand mixer fitted with the paddle attachment, add the butter, cane sugar, and vanilla extract. Mix on low until combined and no chunks of butter remain. Let the mixer mix on low for 5 minutes; set a timer. The butter mixture will look light in color and fluffy.

Add the egg and mix until combined. Add the flour, cinnamon, ginger, and cloves and mix on low until combined into a cookie dough.

Fit a piping bag with the Ateco tip #846 and fill the bag with half the cookie dough. (If you put it in all at once, it can be too hard to squeeze out.) Pipe the dough into 1½-inch dollops onto the prepared baking sheets. Repeat with the remaining half of the dough.

Bake for 10 minutes, or until golden brown around the edges. Sprinkle a little cane sugar on top after coming out of the oven. Let cool completely on the baking sheets.

Store in an airtight container for up to 7 days.

Koloodia Cookies

Makes 40 cookies

My YiaYia ("grandma" in Greek) made these cookies for all the holidays and served them on a silver platter. My entire family called them Koloodia cookies, and it wasn't until I was writing this book that I learned the correct Greek word for them is Koulourakia. The recipe got passed down, and passed down, just like a game of telephone—and so did our name for them! My YiaYia always shaped them in rings, crescents, and twists (as the Greeks do). I would dig through the pile to find the twists, because I thought they tasted best. I still do, so now I make only twists. And I will always call them Koloodias. —MIMI

1 cup water

2 cinnamon sticks

2 cups (452 g) salted butter, softened

1¾ cups (397 g) cane sugar

1 tablespoon plus 1 teaspoon vanilla extract

Scant 5 cups (680 g) cake flour

1⅔ cups plus 2 tablespoons (226 g) all-purpose flour

½ teaspoon baking powder

2 large eggs

〜〜〜 SEA LEVEL 〜〜〜

Bake at 375°F for 20 minutes, or until golden brown on the edges and bottom.

In a small saucepan, add the water and cinnamon sticks and bring to a boil. Once the water has reduced down to ½ cup, remove from the heat. If you boil off too much water, just add some more to bring it back to ½ cup; you want the strong flavor of the cinnamon, so it's better to boil for more time rather than less time. Set aside and let cool completely before beginning the next step.

Preheat the oven to 375°F. Line two baking sheets with parchment paper.

In the bowl of a stand mixer fitted with the paddle attachment, add the butter, cane sugar, and vanilla extract. Mix on low until the ingredients are combined and no chunks of butter remain.

In a separate bowl, add the cake flour, all-purpose flour, and baking powder and whisk together.

Add the eggs and flour mixture to the butter mixture. Start mixing on low, and while continuing to mix, slowly add the cinnamon water until it comes together and forms a smooth dough.

Using your hands, form the dough into 40 balls (each should weigh about 1½ ounces, or 45 grams). Roll them into ropes that are about 7 inches long. Form the rope into a "U" shape and then cross the rope and twist it two times. Place the twisted dough onto the prepared baking sheets, spacing them at least 1 inch apart. (You'll have to reuse the trays, or use more if you have them.)

Bake for 18 minutes, or until golden brown on the edges and bottom. Let cool completely on the baking sheets.

Store in an airtight container for up to 7 days.

Vanilla Bean Biscotti

Makes 12 biscotti

Grab your favorite mug and fill it with an Old-Fashioned Hot Cocoa (page 128) or a
Hot Toddy (page 136), because this biscotti is the perfect dipping vessel! — MIMI

½ cup (113 g) salted butter,
 softened

¾ cup (170 g) cane sugar

2 large eggs

2 cups (255 g) all-purpose flour

1½ teaspoons baking powder

½ teaspoon fine sea salt

½ teaspoon ground vanilla bean

·············· GLUTEN-FREE ··············

Replace the all-purpose flour with
1¾ cups (269 g) gluten-free flour blend.

〜〜〜 SEA LEVEL 〜〜〜

Bake at 350°F for 35 minutes, or until
the middle looks set but not completely
done, then remove and let rest for
10 minutes. Cut and bake again for
20 minutes, or until golden brown,
cracked, and dry on top.

Preheat the oven to 350°F. Line a baking sheet with parchment
paper.

In the bowl of a stand mixer fitted with the paddle attachment,
add the butter and cane sugar. Mix on low until combined and
no chunks of butter remain. Add the eggs and mix just slightly,
enough to break the yolks.

In a separate bowl, add the flour, baking powder, sea salt, and
vanilla bean and whisk together to combine. Add to the butter
mixture and mix on low until combined into a smooth dough.

Using your hands, form the dough into a log so it is almost the
length of the pan; it should be about 13-by-4 inches.

Bake for 30 minutes, or until the middle looks set but not
completely done. Remove from oven and let rest for 10 minutes.

To cut the biscotti: Trim off the smaller edges, then slice into
12 pieces. Space them 1 inch apart and bake for 15 minutes, or
until golden brown, cracked, and dry on top. Let cool completely
on the baking sheet.

Store in a cool, dry place for up to 7 days.

Cookies 'N' Cream Biscotti

Makes 12 biscotti

My husband, Delaney, loves cookies 'n' cream anything. Since part of the joy of baking is sharing with others, I created these biscotti especially for him. His favorite way to eat them is by dipping them in an Old-Fashioned Hot Cocoa (page 128). — MIMI

DOUGH

½ cup (113 g) salted butter, softened

½ cup plus 2 tablespoons (141 g) cane sugar

½ cup (113 g) packed dark brown sugar

2 large eggs

1½ cups (191 g) all-purpose flour

½ cup (43 g) Dutch cocoa powder, sifted

1½ teaspoons baking powder

½ teaspoon fine sea salt

½ teaspoon ground vanilla bean

½ cup (99 g) semi-sweet chocolate chips

TOPPING

8 ounces (226 g) white chocolate, finely chopped

¼ teaspoon ground vanilla bean

.... GLUTEN-FREE ....

Replace the all-purpose flour with 1¼ cups plus 1 tablespoon (205 g) gluten-free flour blend.

〰〰〰 SEA LEVEL 〰〰〰

Bake at 350°F for 35 minutes, until the center looks set but not completely done. Remove from the oven and let rest for 10 minutes. Cut as instructed and bake the biscotti again for 20 minutes, or until cracked and dry on top.

Preheat the oven to 350°F. Line a baking sheet with parchment paper.

To make the dough: In the bowl of a stand mixer fitted with the paddle attachment, add the butter, ½ cup of the cane sugar, and brown sugar. Mix on low until combined and no chunks of butter remain. Add the eggs and mix just slightly, enough to break the yolks.

In a separate bowl, add the flour, cocoa powder, baking powder, sea salt, and ½ teaspoon vanilla bean and whisk together. Add to the butter mixture and mix on low until combined. Add the chocolate chips and mix on low until combined.

Using your hands, form the dough into a log that is about 13-by-4 inches. Place on the prepared baking sheet. Sprinkle the remaining 2 tablespoons cane sugar all over the log.

Bake for 30 minutes, or until the center looks set but not completely done. Remove from the oven and let rest for 10 minutes.

To cut the biscotti: Trim off the smaller edges, then slice into 12 pieces. Space them 1 inch apart and bake for 15 minutes, or until cracked and dry on top. Let cool completely on the baking sheet.

To temper the chocolate: Place about 80 percent of the white chocolate in a heatproof bowl and set aside the remaining 20 percent. To create a double boiler, fill a small saucepan with water and place the bowl with 80 percent of the chocolate on top; do not let the bowl touch the water. Turn on to high heat and melt the chocolate until it reaches 100°F on a digital thermometer. Remove from the heat. Immediately add in the remaining 20 percent of white chocolate and stir vigorously to combine completely. Allow the chocolate to come down to 89°F, then stir in the ¼ teaspoon vanilla bean.

Dip the biscotti into the white chocolate and place them back on the baking sheet. Place the baking sheet in the fridge for 1 hour to set the chocolate.

Store in a cool, dry place for up to 7 days.

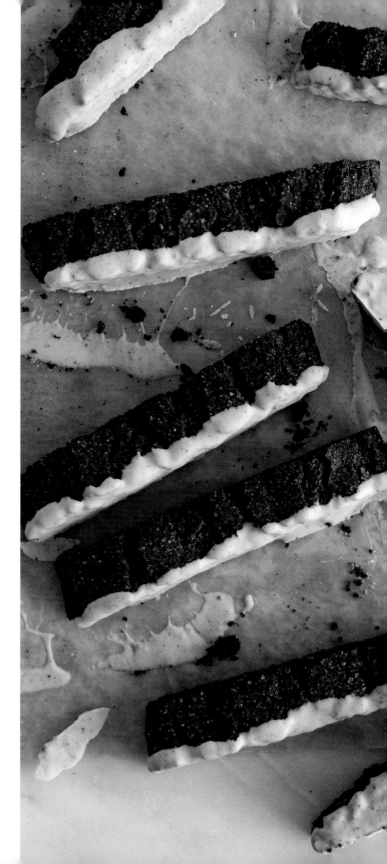

Glazed Five Spice Biscotti

Makes 12 biscotti

If you've never baked with Chinese five spice before, then you are in for a treat. Chinese five spice is a mix of cinnamon, cloves, star anise, fennel, and Szechwan peppercorns. This warm and inviting mix of spices reminds me of Christmas. I remember eating a Christmas cookie with my grandma that had this flavor when I was young, so I always make these for the holidays. Gift this biscotti to friends and family, and it's sure to stand out among the standard gingerbread cookies that everyone normally receives. — **MIMI**

DOUGH

½ cup (113 g) salted butter, softened

½ cup (113 g) cane sugar

¼ cup (57 g) packed dark brown sugar

2 large eggs

2 cups (255 g) all-purpose flour

2 teaspoons Chinese five spice

½ teaspoon ground vanilla bean

½ teaspoon baking soda

½ teaspoon fine sea salt

GLAZE

1 cup (142 g) powdered sugar, sifted

2 tablespoons (30 ml) milk

·········· **GLUTEN-FREE** ··········

Replace the all-purpose flour with 1¾ cups (269 g) gluten-free flour blend.

〜〜〜 **SEA LEVEL** 〜〜〜

Bake at 350°F for 35 minutes, or until the middle looks set but not completely done, then remove and let rest for 10 minutes. Cut as instructed and bake again for 20 minutes, or until golden brown, cracked, and dry on top.

Preheat the oven to 350°F. Line a baking sheet with parchment paper.

To make the dough: In the bowl of a stand mixer fitted with the paddle attachment, add the butter, cane sugar, and brown sugar. Mix on low until all ingredients are combined and no chunks of butter remain. Add the eggs and mix just slightly, enough to break the yolks.

In a separate bowl, add the flour, Chinese five spice, vanilla bean, baking soda, and sea salt and whisk together to combine. Add to the butter mixture and mix on low until combined into a smooth dough.

Using your hands, form the dough into a log so it is almost the length of the pan; it should be about 13-by-4 inches. Bake for 30 minutes, or until the middle looks set but not completely done. Remove from the oven and let rest for 10 minutes.

To cut the biscotti: Trim off the smaller edges, then slice into 12 pieces. Space them 1 inch apart and bake for 15 minutes, or until golden brown, cracked, and dry on top. Let cool completely on baking sheet.

To make the glaze: In a mixing bowl, add the powdered sugar and milk, and whisk together until smooth. Drizzle over the top of the biscotti.

Store in a cool, dry place for up to 7 days.

London Fog Blondies

Makes 9 bars

A London Fog is a hot drink with Earl Grey tea, vanilla, and steamed milk.
The sweet vanilla flavor made me think it would be delicious as a dessert, so I
created a blondie version. And here it is. — MIMI

BATTER

3 bags Earl Grey tea

2 cups (255 g) all-purpose flour

Scant ½ cup (43 g) coconut flour

½ teaspoon baking powder

½ teaspoon fine sea salt

1 cup (226 g) cane sugar

2 ounces (57 g) white
  chocolate, finely chopped

1 cup (240 ml) water

⅓ cup (80 ml) canola oil

1 large egg

1 teaspoon vanilla extract

ICING

1¼ cups (185 g) powdered sugar,
  sifted

2 tablespoons (28 g) salted
  butter, softened

¼ cup (60 ml) heavy
  whipping cream

½ teaspoon vanilla extract

.... GLUTEN-FREE ....

Replace the all-purpose flour with
1⅔ cups (255 g) gluten-free flour blend.

〜〜〜 SEA LEVEL 〜〜〜

Follow the recipe as noted.

Preheat the oven to 350°F. Line a 9-by-9-inch baking pan with
parchment paper.

To make the batter: Open 2 of the tea bags and empty the
contents into a medium bowl. Add the flour, coconut flour, baking
powder, and sea salt and whisk together. Set aside.

In the bowl of a stand mixer fitted with the paddle attachment,
add the cane sugar and white chocolate. Set aside.

In a small saucepan, add the remaining tea bag and the water.
Bring to a boil. Add ½ cup of the brewed tea into the mixing bowl
with the cane sugar and white chocolate. Mix on low immediately
until the hot tea has melted the white chocolate.

Add in the canola oil, egg, and 1 teaspoon vanilla extract. Mix on
low until combined. Add the flour mixture and mix on low until
combined.

Transfer the batter into the prepared baking pan and spread
evenly. Bake for 24 minutes, or until a toothpick inserted in the
center comes out clean. Let cool completely. Once cooled, cut
around the edges and remove in one piece from the baking pan.

To make the icing: In the bowl of a stand mixer fitted with the
paddle attachment, add the powdered sugar, butter, whipping
cream, and ½ teaspoon vanilla extract. Mix on low until
combined, then speed up the mixer to high for 1 minute, or until
light and fluffy. Spread the icing over the top of the blondies. Cut
into nine bars.

Store in an airtight container for up to 7 days.

Double Black Diamond Brownies

Makes 9 brownies

During our annual ski vacations growing up, the goal was always to ski the entire mountain. To make it through the day, my dad would sometimes bribe me with a treat. This was a great motivator, and it was always a victory for me when I skied all the double black diamond runs. I have added activated charcoal to these brownies to give them a black tint—all you have to do is tilt them to make them look like diamonds. I would have loved this as a victory treat for conquering the mountain. — MIMI

BATTER

2 cups (255 g) all-purpose flour

1 tablespoon (8 g)
 activated charcoal

½ teaspoon baking powder

½ teaspoon sea salt

½ teaspoon vanilla bean

1¼ cups (284 g) cane sugar

½ cup (113 g) coconut oil

2 ounces (57 g) dark chocolate,
 finely chopped

⅔ cup (57 g) Dutch cocoa
 powder, sifted

½ cup boiling water

¼ cup unsweetened
 vanilla coconut milk

GANACHE

8 ounces (226 g) dark
 chocolate, finely chopped

½ cup plus 2 tablespoons
 (150 g) coconut cream

¼ teaspoon peppermint flavor

.... GLUTEN-FREE ....

Replace the all-purpose flour with
1⅔ cups (255 g) gluten-free flour blend.

⌒⌒⌒ SEA LEVEL ⌒⌒⌒

Bake at 350°F for 23 minutes,
or until a toothpick inserted in the
center comes out clean.

Preheat the oven to 350°F. Line a 9-by-9-inch baking pan with parchment paper.

To make the batter: In a medium bowl, add the flour, activated charcoal, baking powder, sea salt, and vanilla bean and whisk together. Set aside.

In the bowl of a stand mixer fitted with the paddle attachment, add the cane sugar, coconut oil, dark chocolate, and cocoa powder. Add the boiling water and mix on medium speed until all the chocolate and cocoa are melted and you have a smooth chocolate.

Add in the coconut milk and the flour mixture and mix on low until combined; do not overmix. Fold a few times with a spatula if you still see bits of flour.

Transfer the batter into the prepared pan. You will have to spread it out until the brownie batter is completely even. Bake for 18 minutes, or until a toothpick inserted in the center comes out clean. Let cool completely. Once cooled, cut around the edges and remove in one piece from the baking pan.

To make the ganache: In a double boiler, add the dark chocolate and melt it completely. Add the coconut cream and stir to combine completely; remove from the heat. Add in the peppermint flavor and stir to combine completely. Allow to cool to room temperature.

Add the chocolate ganache into the bowl of a stand mixer fitted with the whisk attachment. Whisk on low then gradually increase speed to high until the chocolate is fluffy. Spread over the top of the brownies. Cut into nine squares.

Store in an airtight container in the fridge for up to 7 days.

CAKES & PIES

After establishing Dessert'D, we started to get many requests for cakes, so I knew fairly early on that I would soon be selling cakes in addition to cookies. Shortly after we created our cake menu, we were flooded with requests for pies as well. Pies inevitably made their way to our menu, too. Truth be told, cakes and pies are desserts that I have always liked, but I was never inspired to bake on my own until I was commissioned to do so. But I'm so glad for these opportunities, because I soon fell in love with the different processes and techniques of both cake and pie baking.

Once I got in the kitchen and actually started baking and frosting cakes and rolling out pie dough, the inspiration came. Yes, cakes and pies take a little more time than cookies. And yes, the techniques take a little more practice. Add the challenge of making picture-perfect cakes, and let's just say I haven't been bored since. When I want something a little more rustic and free-form and yet equally delicious, I make a galette.

I hope this chapter leads you to your kitchen and inspires you to bake something a little different than what you're used to making. Indulge at breakfast with Coffee Cake (page 206) and impress your friends and family with Chocolate Sage Pecan Cake (page 221). Step out of your comfort zone and bake a Zucchini Loaf (page 201), instead of your usual banana bread. The recipes in this chapter are not only unique, they are also designed to teach you techniques that you'll use forever to hone your baking skills. —MIMI

Zucchini Loaf

Makes one 9-by-5-inch loaf cake

During the summer months, my mom would sometimes bring home a loaf of
zucchini bread from a local bakery. It was moist, a little spicy, and filled with
walnuts. We would slather butter on top of it and eat it for dessert. At high altitude,
it's difficult to add things like walnuts into cakes because they usually sink, so I
created a zucchini loaf cake with a buttercream icing and added the walnuts on top.
It's perfect for dessert or for wrapping up and taking on the trail. —MIMI

BATTER

6 ounces (170 g) zucchini,
  finely grated

½ cup (120 ml) canola oil

¼ cup plus 2 tablespoons (85 g)
  packed dark brown sugar

¼ cup plus 2 tablespoons
  (85 g) cane sugar

2 large eggs

1⅓ cups (170 g) all-purpose flour

1 teaspoon cinnamon

1 teaspoon baking powder

½ teaspoon cloves

½ teaspoon fine sea salt

ICING

1 cup (142 g) powdered sugar, sifted

¼ cup (57 g) salted butter, softened

1 tablespoon heavy whipping cream

½ teaspoon vanilla extract

TOPPING

¾ cup (85 g) chopped walnuts

.... GLUTEN-FREE ....

Replace the all-purpose flour with 1 cup
plus 1 tablespoon plus 1 teaspoon (170 g)
gluten-free flour blend.

～～～ SEA LEVEL ～～～

Bake at 350°F for 1 hour 15 minutes, or
until a toothpick inserted in the center
comes out clean.

Preheat the oven to 350°F. Line a 9-by-5-inch loaf pan with
parchment paper, letting it fold over the sides for easier removal.

To make the batter: In the bowl of a stand mixer fitted with the
paddle attachment, add the zucchini, canola oil, brown sugar,
cane sugar, and eggs. Mix on low until combined.

In a separate bowl, add the flour, cinnamon, baking powder,
cloves, and sea salt and whisk together. Add to the zucchini
mixture and mix on low until combined.

Transfer the batter to the prepared pan. Bake for 1 hour, or until
a toothpick inserted in the center comes out clean. Allow the cake
to cool completely before removing.

To make the icing: In the bowl of a stand mixer fitted with the
paddle attachment, add the powdered sugar, butter, whipping
cream, and vanilla extract. Mix on low until combined, then speed
up the mixer to high for 1 minute, or until light and fluffy.

Using a spatula, spread the icing over the top of the cake. Sprinkle
with walnuts.

Store in an airtight container for up to 3 days.

Strawberry Shortcake

Makes one 9-inch cake

One of my favorite childhood memories is dining alfresco on our patio. Even though I lived in Chicago as a child and we didn't have mountain views, eating dinner outside just always made it better. It might have also been better because my mom usually served dessert. One of her go-to summer desserts was strawberry shortcake. This is my version, and it always makes me think fondly of warm summer nights with my family. Now, I just have better views. — MIMI

3 (102 g) large egg whites

½ cup (113 g) salted butter, softened

¾ cup plus 2 tablespoons (198 g) cane sugar

1 teaspoon vanilla extract

½ cup (120 ml) milk

1 cup plus 3 tablespoons (170 g) cake flour

1 teaspoon baking powder

½ teaspoon fine sea salt

Whipped Cream (page 131)

Fresh strawberries

.... GLUTEN-FREE ....

Replace the cake flour with 1 cup plus 1 tablespoon plus 1 teaspoon (170 g) gluten-free flour blend.

~~~~~ SEA LEVEL ~~~~~

Bake at 350°F for 35 minutes, or until a toothpick inserted in the center comes out clean.

Preheat the oven to 350°F.

In the bowl of a stand mixer fitted with the whisk attachment, add the egg whites. Whisk, starting on low to avoid splattering; gradually increase the speed to high until stiff peaks form. Remove the egg whites from the mixing bowl and transfer to a separate bowl. Set aside.

In the bowl of the stand mixer fitted with the whisk attachment (no need to wash the bowl), add the butter, cane sugar, and vanilla extract. Mix on low until combined and no chunks of butter remain. Add the milk and mix on low until combined, scraping down the sides of the bowl as needed.

In a separate bowl, add the cake flour, baking powder, and sea salt and whisk together. With the mixer on low, slowly add the cake flour mixture to the butter mixture and continue to mix on low until combined, scraping down the sides of the bowl as needed.

Remove the bowl from the stand mixer and add in the egg whites; fold with a spatula until you have a smooth batter.

Line a 9-inch cake pan with parchment paper, and butter and flour the sides. Pour the batter into the cake pan and spread evenly. Bake for 30 minutes, or until a toothpick inserted in the center comes out clean. Allow the cake to cool completely before removing it from the pan.

Top with Whipped Cream and strawberries. Store in an airtight container in the fridge for up to 3 days.

Poppy Seed Pound Cake

Makes one 9-by-5-inch loaf cake

I've been obsessed with pound cake since I was a little girl, so I'm constantly creating different kinds. If this type of cake is new to you, get ready to have a new favorite. Pound cake is sweet and dense, and the crust is actually the best part. Our regular customers at Dessert'D know to ask for the end slices when we make this loaf in the bake shop. — MIMI

BATTER

½ cup (113 g) salted butter, softened

1½ cups (340 g) cane sugar

1½ teaspoons almond flavor

1 teaspoon vanilla extract

3 large eggs

½ cup (120 ml) milk

1½ cups (212 g) cake flour

½ teaspoon fine sea salt

1 tablespoon (10 g) poppy seeds

Canola oil cooking spray

ICING

1 ounce (28 g) dark chocolate, finely chopped

¼ cup (57 g) salted butter, softened

1 cup (142 g) powdered sugar, sifted

1 tablespoon (15 ml) heavy whipping cream

········· GLUTEN-FREE ·········

Replace the cake flour with 1 cup plus 3 tablespoons (184 g) gluten-free flour blend and ¼ cup plus 1 tablespoon (28 g) coconut flour.

〜〜〜 SEA LEVEL 〜〜〜

Bake at 350°F for 1 hour 30 minutes, or until a toothpick inserted in the center comes out clean.

Preheat the oven to 350°F. Line a 9-by-5-inch loaf pan with parchment paper, letting it fold over the sides for easier removal.

To make the batter: In the bowl of a stand mixer fitted with the paddle attachment, add the ½ cup butter, cane sugar, almond flavor, and vanilla extract. Mix on low until no chunks of butter remain.

Add the eggs and milk and mix on low until combined, scraping down the sides so there are no butter chunks.

In a separate bowl, add the cake flour and sea salt, and whisk together. With the mixer on low, slowly add the flour mixture to the butter mixture and continue to mix on low until you have a smooth batter. Add the poppy seeds and mix until combined, scraping down the sides of the bowl as needed.

Grease the loaf pan well with canola oil cooking spray. Pour the batter into the prepared pan and spread out evenly. Bake for 1 hour 15 minutes, or until a toothpick inserted in the center comes out clean. Allow the cake to cool completely before removing.

To make the icing: Melt the dark chocolate in a double boiler. Remove from the heat. In the bowl of a stand mixer fitted with the paddle attachment, add the ¼ cup butter, powdered sugar, melted dark chocolate, and heavy whipping cream. Mix on low until combined, and then speed up the mixer to high for 1 minute or until light and fluffy.

Spread the icing over the top of the cake.

Store in an airtight container or a cake dome for up to 3 days.

Coffee Cake

Makes one 9-inch cake

Every Christmas we enjoyed coffee cake from a local bakery, and I savored every single piece. My mom loved having a coffee cake around because it made breakfast quick and easy. And on Christmas morning that was essential because we wanted to spend time with each other. You can easily make this cake ahead of time so it's ready for the next morning. —MIMI

BATTER

½ cup (113 g) salted butter

½ cup (113 g) packed dark brown sugar

¼ cup (57 g) cane sugar

1 teaspoon vanilla extract

1 teaspoon coffee flavor

2 large eggs

¼ cup (57 g) sour cream

¼ cup (60 ml) milk

1½ cups (212 g) cake flour

½ teaspoon baking powder

½ teaspoon fine sea salt

TOPPING

¾ cup (95 g) all-purpose flour

¼ cup plus 2 tablespoons (85 g) packed dark brown sugar

2 tablespoons (28 g) cane sugar

1½ teaspoons cinnamon

6 tablespoons (85 g) salted butter, melted

GLAZE

½ cup (71 g) powdered sugar, sifted

2 tablespoons (30 ml) water

To brown the butter: Add the butter to a small saucepan over medium heat. Allow the butter to melt, stirring occasionally. Once the butter has completely melted, it will start to brown. It may bubble up and turn white, which will make it hard to see the color. If this happens, remove from the heat until the bubbles calm down, and return to heat if it's not done. When it's done the butter will be a light brown color, similar to maple syrup. The milk solids will also sink to the bottom and form small darker specs. This can take 5 to 10 minutes; be sure to remove the butter from the heat as soon as it has browned, as it can burn quickly. Allow to cool completely before beginning next step.

Preheat the oven to 375°F. Line a 9-inch cake pan with parchment paper.

To make the batter: In the bowl of a stand mixer fitted with the paddle attachment, add the brown butter, ½ cup brown sugar, ¼ cup cane sugar, vanilla extract, and coffee flavor. Mix on low until combined and no chunks of butter remain. Add the eggs, sour cream, and milk and mix on low until combined.

In a separate bowl, add the cake flour, baking powder, and sea salt and whisk together. With the mixer on low, slowly add the cake flour mixture to the butter mixture and continue to mix on low until combined into a smooth batter, scraping down the sides of the bowl as needed.

Pour the batter into the prepared cake pan and spread out evenly. Bake for 15 minutes. Set a timer. While the cake is baking, get the topping ready.

To make the topping: Add the all-purpose flour, ¼ cup plus 2 tablespoons brown sugar, 2 tablespoons cane sugar, and cinnamon to a medium bowl and swirl together. Add the

6 tablespoons melted butter and fold together with a spatula until you have a paste.

Once the timer goes off, remove the cake from the oven and using your hands, crumble the topping onto the partially baked cake batter. Return the cake to the oven and bake for 20 minutes, or until a toothpick inserted in the center comes out clean. Allow the cake to cool completely before removing from the pan.

To make the glaze: Add the powdered sugar and water into a small bowl and whisk together. Using a pastry brush, brush the glaze on top of the cake.

Store in an airtight container for up to 7 days.

·········· **GLUTEN-FREE** ··········

Replace the cake flour with 1⅓ cups (212 g) gluten-free flour blend and replace the all-purpose flour with ½ cup plus 1 tablespoon (95 g) gluten-free flour blend.

〰〰〰 **SEA LEVEL** 〰〰〰

Bake at 375°F for 20 minutes. After the topping is added, bake for 20 minutes, or until a toothpick inserted in the center comes out clean.

Chocolate Pound Cake

Makes one 10-inch Bundt cake

When I graduated high school early to move to Mammoth Lakes, California, I had a dessert party in lieu of a traditional graduation party. I made every single dessert myself, so of course I had multiple pound cakes at my party. No matter the occasion, you can't go wrong with a classic chocolate pound cake, and I think this one is particularly spectacular. — MIMI

1 cup (227 g) salted butter, softened

1½ cups (340 g) cane sugar

1½ cups (340 g) packed dark brown sugar

6 large eggs

1 cup (120 ml) heavy cream

2⅔ cups (369 g) cake flour

⅔ cup (57 g) Dutch cocoa powder, sifted

1 teaspoon ground vanilla bean

½ teaspoon fine sea salt

Canola oil cooking spray

Powdered sugar for dusting

.... GLUTEN-FREE ....

Replace the cake flour with 2 cups (310 g) gluten-free flour blend and ½ cup (49 g) coconut flour.

SEA LEVEL

Bake at 350°F for 2 hours 15 minutes, or until a toothpick inserted in the center comes out clean.

Preheat the oven to 350°F.

In the bowl of a stand mixer fitted with the paddle attachment, add the butter, cane sugar, and brown sugar. Mix on low until combined and no chunks of butter remain. Add in the eggs and cream and mix on low until combined.

In a separate bowl, add the cake flour, cocoa, vanilla bean, and sea salt and whisk together. With the mixer on low, slowly add the flour mixture and continue to mix on low until combined into a smooth batter, scraping down the sides of the bowl as needed.

Grease a 10-inch Bundt pan with canola oil cooking spray. Pour the cake batter into the Bundt pan. Bake for 1 hour 45 minutes, or until a toothpick inserted in the center comes out clean.

Allow the cake to cool completely before removing. Place on a cake stand or plate and sift the powdered sugar on top.

Store in an airtight container or a cake dome for up to 7 days.

Lemon Pistachio Pound Cake

Makes one 10-inch Bundt cake

Pound cakes are great to bake ahead of time because they can stay tucked away inside the Bundt pan until they are ready to be served. This alleviates having to cover it or store it in an airtight container or dome, as you would any other type of cake. I always bake my pound cakes at night, then take them out of the oven and let them cool overnight on the counter. The next day, I know they are cool enough to remove from the pan, frost, and serve. — MIMI

BATTER

1 cup (226 grams) salted butter, softened

3 cups (680 g) cane sugar

2 teaspoons pistachio extract

6 large eggs

1 cup (120 ml) milk

3 cups (425 g) cake flour

½ teaspoon fine sea salt

Canola oil cooking spray

GLAZE

2 cups (284 g) powdered sugar, sifted

Juice of 1 large lemon

TOPPING

¼ cup (35 g) finely chopped pistachios, roasted, salted, and shelled

············ GLUTEN-FREE ············

Replace the cake flour with 2⅔ cups plus 1 teaspoon (369 g) gluten-free flour blend and ½ cup plus 1 tablespoon (57 g) coconut flour.

〰〰〰 SEA LEVEL 〰〰〰

Bake at 350°F for 2 hours 15 minutes, or until a toothpick inserted in the center comes out clean.

Preheat the oven to 350°F.

To make the batter: In the bowl of a stand mixer fitted with the paddle attachment, add the butter, cane sugar, and pistachio extract. Mix on low until combined and no chunks of butter remain. Add in the eggs and milk and mix on low until combined.

In a separate bowl, add the cake flour and sea salt and whisk together. With the mixer on low, slowly add the cake flour mixture to the butter mixture, scraping down the sides of the bowl as needed.

Grease a 10-inch Bundt pan with canola oil cooking spray. Pour the cake batter into the Bundt pan. Bake for 1 hour 45 minutes, or until a toothpick inserted in the center comes out clean. Allow cake to cool completely before removing.

To make the glaze: Add the powdered sugar and lemon juice to a medium mixing bowl. Whisk until combined into a smooth glaze.

Place the cake on a cake stand or plate and pour the frosting over the top of the cake so it runs down the sides. Top with the pistachios.

Store in an airtight container or a cake dome for up to 7 days.

Raspberry Mint Galette

Makes one 9-inch galette

Galette is a word used in French baking to describe flat cakes or pies. Basically, it's a pie with no dish. This makes them easier to bake because you don't have to worry about forming perfect pie dough. You just roll it out and fold it up; it's really that simple. With no pie dish to wash afterward, it's my kind of baking. — MIMI

CRUST

1 cup (127 g) all-purpose flour

1 teaspoon cane sugar

½ cup (113 g) salted butter, cold

3 tablespoons (45 ml) cold water

1 small egg

FILLING

¼ cup plus 2 tablespoons (85 g) cane sugar

2 tablespoons (15 g) all-purpose flour

1 teaspoon cornstarch

2 cups (283 g) fresh raspberries

Powdered sugar for garnish

Fresh mint leaves for garnish

~~~ SEA LEVEL ~~~

Bake at 350°F for 1 hour, or until golden brown.

To make the crust: In the bowl of a stand mixer fitted with the paddle attachment, add the 1 cup flour and 1 teaspoon cane sugar. Turn the mixer on low for two to three rotations to combine the dry ingredients.

Remove the butter from the fridge and chop into small cubes. The smaller the cubes, the flakier the crust: Cut the stick of butter into four and then chop into small cubes from there. Add the cold, cubed butter to the flour mixture. Measure out the cold water and have it ready.

Turn the mixer on low and slowly start to incorporate the ingredients. Gradually turn the mixer to medium speed. Once the butter mixture looks like wet sand, immediately add in all the water. As soon as the dough comes together, stop the mixer.

Form the dough into a disk and wrap in plastic wrap. Allow to cool in the fridge for at least 6 hours or overnight.

Preheat the oven to 350°F. Line a baking sheet with parchment paper. Remove the dough from the fridge. In a small dish, beat the egg and set aside.

To make the filling: In a medium bowl, add the ¼ cup plus 2 tablespoons cane sugar, 2 tablespoons flour, and cornstarch and whisk together. Add the raspberries and toss to coat completely. Set aside.

On a floured surface, roll out the dough to ¼-inch thick; it should measure about 12 inches in diameter. Place the circle of dough onto the prepared baking sheet. Add the filling to the middle of the dough and spread it out, leaving a border of dough of about 2 inches.

Fold over the remaining border of dough into the middle to create a crust. Brush the edges of the dough with the egg wash using a pastry brush. Bake for 45 minutes, or until golden brown.

To serve, dust with powdered sugar and top with fresh mint leaves.

Store in a cool, dry place for up to 3 days.

Glazed Blueberry Galette

Makes one 9-inch galette

This galette can be enjoyed morning, noon, or night. And it's easy to make all year round because you can use frozen blueberries if you can't get fresh. Just leave them in a strainer overnight (in the fridge) to drain off excess moisture. — MIMI

CRUST

1 cup (127 g) all-purpose flour

1 teaspoon cane sugar

½ cup (113 g) salted butter, cold

3 tablespoons (45 ml) cold water

1 small egg

FILLING

¼ cup plus 2 tablespoons (85 g) cane sugar

2 tablespoons (15 g) all-purpose flour

1 teaspoon cornstarch

¼ teaspoon cinnamon

1½ cups (255 g) fresh blueberries

GLAZE

½ cup (71 g) powdered sugar, sifted

2 teaspoons apple juice

Pinch of ginger

〜〜〜 SEA LEVEL 〜〜〜

Bake at 350°F for 1 hour, or until golden brown.

To make the crust: In the bowl of a stand mixer fitted with the paddle attachment, add the 1 cup flour and 1 teaspoon cane sugar. Turn the mixer on low for two to three rotations to combine the dry ingredients.

Remove the butter from the fridge and chop into small cubes. The smaller the cubes, the flakier the crust: Cut the stick of butter into four and then chop into small cubes from there. Add the cold, cubed butter to the flour mixture. Measure out the cold water and have it ready.

Turn the mixer on low and slowly start to incorporate the ingredients. Gradually turn the mixer to medium speed. Once the butter mixture looks like wet sand, immediately add in all the water. As soon as the dough comes together, stop the mixer.

Form the dough into a disk and wrap in plastic wrap. Allow to cool in the fridge for at least 6 hours or overnight.

Preheat the oven to 350°F. Line a baking sheet with parchment paper. Remove the dough from the fridge. In a small dish, beat the egg and set aside.

To make the filling: In a medium bowl, add the ¼ cup plus 2 tablespoons cane sugar, 2 tablespoons flour, cornstarch, and cinnamon and whisk together to combine. Add the blueberries and coat them completely in the flour mixture. Set aside.

On a floured surface, roll out the dough to ¼-inch thick; it should measure about 12 inches in diameter. Place the circle of dough onto the prepared baking sheet. Add the filling to the middle of the dough and spread out, leaving a border of dough of about 2 inches.

Fold over the remaining border of dough into the middle to create a crust. Brush the edges of the dough with the egg wash using a pastry brush. Bake for 45 minutes, or until golden brown.

To make the glaze: Add the powdered sugar, apple juice, and ginger into a medium bowl. Whisk together until smooth. Drizzle over the top of the galette.

Store in a cool, dry place for up to 3 days.

Chocolate Peanut Butter Pecan Galette

Makes one 9-inch galette

Move over pecan pie. This is the hot (*pun intended*) new dessert for Thanksgiving and Christmas! Chocolate, peanut butter, pecans, cinnamon—what more could you want from a rustic take on pecan pie? Not only is this galette super easy to make, it will wow everyone at your mountain house with its similarities to the classic pecan pie . . . but with a bold flavor profile, not to mention chocolate and peanut butter! —MIMI

DOUGH

1 cup (127 g) all-purpose flour

1 teaspoon cane sugar

½ cup (113 g) salted butter, cold

3 tablespoons (45 ml) cold water

1 small egg

FILLING

1 cup (127 g) pecan halves

¼ cup (21 g) Dutch cocoa powder, sifted

¼ teaspoon cinnamon

¼ cup (57 g) packed dark brown sugar

¼ cup (57 g) cane sugar

¼ cup (35 g) finely chopped milk chocolate

2 tablespoons (28 g) salted butter

1 teaspoon light corn syrup

¼ cup (71 g) peanut butter

1 large egg

〰〰〰 SEA LEVEL 〰〰〰

Bake at 350°F for 1 hour, or until golden brown.

To make the crust: In the bowl of a stand mixer fitted with the paddle attachment, add the flour and 1 teaspoon cane sugar. Turn the mixer on low for two to three rotations to combine the dry ingredients.

Remove the ½ cup butter from the fridge and chop into small cubes. The smaller the cubes, the flakier the crust: Cut the stick of butter into four and then chop into small cubes from there. Add the cold cubed butter to the flour mixture. Measure out the cold water and have it ready.

Turn the mixer on low and slowly start to incorporate the ingredients. Gradually turn the mixer to medium speed. Once the butter mixture looks like wet sand, immediately add in all the water. As soon as the dough comes together, stop the mixer.

Form the dough into a disk and wrap in plastic wrap. Allow to cool in the fridge for at least 6 hours or overnight.

Preheat the oven to 350°F. Line a baking sheet with parchment paper.

Remove the dough from the fridge. In a small dish, beat the small egg and set aside.

On a floured surface, roll out the dough to ¼-inch thick; it should measure about 12 inches in diameter. Place the circle of dough onto the prepared baking sheet.

To make the filling: In a medium bowl, add the pecans, cocoa powder, and cinnamon. Mix together and set aside.

In a small saucepan, add the brown sugar, ¼ cup cane sugar, milk chocolate, 2 tablespoons butter, and corn syrup. Put over

medium heat and melt. Once completely combined, remove from the heat.

Add the brown sugar mixture to the pecans and stir to combine completely. Add the peanut butter and large egg and stir to combine completely. Add the filling to the middle of the dough and spread out, leaving a border of dough of about 2 inches.

Fold over the remaining border of dough into the middle to create a crust. Brush the edges of the dough with the egg wash using a pastry brush. Bake for 45 minutes, or until golden brown.

Store in a cool, dry place for up to 3 days.

Spiced Apple Mini Pies

Makes 6 mini pies

These mini pies are actually galettes, because they are made sans pie dish. This is how we make our mini pies at Dessert'D, because we can make a lot when needed and we don't have to clean tons of little dishes. If you have 5-inch pie dishes, however, you can certainly use them to bake these mini pies. — MIMI

CRUST

2 cups (255 g) all-purpose flour

½ teaspoon cane sugar

¼ teaspoon cinnamon

¾ cup (170 g) salted butter, cold

½ cup (120 ml) cold water

1 large egg

FILLING

½ cup (113 g) cane sugar

3 tablespoons (43 g) packed dark brown sugar

2 tablespoons (17 g) all-purpose flour

¼ teaspoon cinnamon

¼ teaspoon ginger

¼ teaspoon cloves

2 large apples (Fuji, Gala, or Cripps Pink)

GLAZE

¾ cup (106 g) powdered sugar, sifted

1½ tablespoons (22 ml) water

〰〰 SEA LEVEL 〰〰

Bake at 350°F for 50 minutes, or until golden brown.

To make the crust: In the bowl of a stand mixer fitted with the paddle attachment, add the 2 cups flour, ½ teaspoon cane sugar, and ¼ teaspoon cinnamon. Turn on low for two to three rotations to combine the dry ingredients.

Remove the butter from the fridge and chop into small cubes. The smaller the cubes, the flakier the crust: Cut the stick of butter into four and then chop into small cubes from there. Add the cold, cubed butter to the flour mixture. Measure out the cold water and have it ready.

Turn the mixer on low and slowly start to incorporate the ingredients. Gradually turn the mixer to medium speed. Once the butter mixture looks like wet sand, immediately add in all the ½ cup cold water. As soon as the dough comes together, stop the mixer.

Have six pieces of plastic wrap ready. Divide the dough into six pieces, weighing about 3 ounces (85 grams) each. Form each piece of dough into a disk and wrap in plastic wrap. Allow to cool in the fridge for at least 4 hours or overnight before rolling out the pies.

Preheat the oven to 350°F. Line two baking sheets with parchment paper. In a small bowl, beat the egg and set aside.

To make the filling: In a medium bowl, add the ½ cup cane sugar, brown sugar, 2 tablespoons flour, ¼ teaspoon cinnamon, ginger, and cloves, and whisk together to combine completely. Chop the apples into thin slices, leaving on the skins. Add to the sugar mixture and toss to coat completely.

(continued)

Remove the plastic wrap from the six dough disks and place them on a floured surface. Roll out to ¼-inch thick, about 7 inches in diameter. Transfer them to the prepared baking sheets.

Place a generous amount of filling into the middle of each dough, leaving about a 1-inch border. Fold the border into the middle to create a crust. Using a pastry brush, brush the crust of each mini pie with the egg wash.

Bake for 45 minutes, or until golden brown. Let cool completely on the baking sheets.

To make the glaze: In a small bowl, add the powdered sugar and 1½ tablespoons water and whisk together until smooth. Drizzle over the tops of each pie.

Store in a cool, dry place for up to 3 days.

Chocolate Sage Pecan Cake

Makes a three-layer 6-inch cake

Chocolate has always been my favorite kind of cake, and I'm constantly looking for ways to make it interesting. I have covered the outside of this cake with sage pecans, which you can also make as a stand-alone snack. — MIMI

BATTER

½ cup (113 g) salted butter, softened

¾ cup (170 g) cane sugar

1 teaspoon vanilla extract

2 large eggs

½ cup (120 ml) milk

¼ cup (57 g) sour cream

¾ cup plus 2½ tablespoons (127 g) cake flour

½ cup (43 g) Dutch cocoa powder, sifted

¾ teaspoon baking powder

½ teaspoon fine sea salt

TOPPING

2 tablespoons (28 g) coconut oil

2 tablespoons (28 g) cane sugar

2 teaspoons finely chopped fresh sage

¾ cup (96 g) pecan halves

FROSTING

3 cups (425 g) powdered sugar, sifted

1 cup (226 g) salted butter, softened

⅓ cup (28 g) Dutch cocoa powder, sifted

2 to 3 teaspoons (10 to 15 ml) milk

Preheat the oven to 350°F. Line three 6-inch cake pans with parchment paper.

To make the batter: In the bowl of a stand mixer fitted with the paddle attachment, add the ½ cup butter, ¾ cup cane sugar, and vanilla extract and mix on low until combined and no chunks of butter remain. Add the eggs and mix on low until combined. Add the milk and sour cream and mix for one to two rotations.

In a separate bowl, add the cake flour, ½ cup cocoa powder, baking powder, and sea salt and whisk together. With the mixer on low, slowly add the flour mixture to the butter mixture until a smooth batter forms, scraping down the sides of the bowl as needed.

Transfer the batter into the prepared cake pans evenly, about 8 ounces (226 grams) each. Bake for 17 minutes, or until a toothpick inserted in the center comes out clean. Allow to cool completely before removing.

To make the topping: Line a baking sheet with parchment paper. Add the coconut oil, 2 tablespoons cane sugar, and fresh sage into a small saucepan. Put the pan over medium heat and allow the coconut oil to melt. Then add in the pecans and cook for 2 to 4 minutes, until the aroma is fragrant and the pecans look toasted. Transfer the pecans to the prepared baking sheet and let cool until the coconut oil has solidified. (You can even pop the baking sheet into the freezer to speed up the process.)

(continued)

To make the frosting: In the bowl of a stand mixer fitted with the paddle attachment, add the powdered sugar, 1 cup butter, ⅓ cup cocoa powder, and 2 teaspoons milk. Mix on low until combined then speed up the mixer to high for 1 minute more, or until light and fluffy. If the frosting seems dry, then add more milk, 1 teaspoon at a time, and continue to mix on high until light and fluffy.

On a cake stand or spinner, place the first cake layer and using a cake spatula, place a generous amount of frosting and spread evenly. Place the second cake layer on top and repeat this process. Place the last cake layer and frost the cake with the remaining frosting. Decorate the outside and top of the cake with the pecan topping.

Store in an airtight container or a cake dome for up to 3 days.

Snow Day Cake

Makes a two-layer 6-inch cake

This is the kind of cake I want to bake while staying home on a snow day. If you are new to cake baking, this is a great recipe to start with because the outside is entirely covered in coconut flakes. This means you can practice your frosting skills without worry, because the flakes will cover your tracks. This cake pairs wonderfully with Old-Fashioned Hot Cocoa (page 128). — **MIMI**

BATTER

½ cup (113 g) salted
  butter, softened

¾ cup (170 g) cane sugar

1 teaspoon almond extract

2 large eggs

¼ cup (60 ml) milk

¼ cup (60 ml) unsweetened
  vanilla coconut milk

1 cup plus 3 tablespoons
  (170 g) cake flour

¾ teaspoon baking powder

½ teaspoon cardamom

½ teaspoon fine sea salt

FROSTING

¾ cup (170 g) salted
  butter, softened

Heaping 2⅓ cups (340 g)
  powdered sugar, sifted

1 teaspoon vanilla extract

TOPPING

½ cup (45 g) unsweetened
  fine shredded coconut

············ **GLUTEN-FREE** ············

Replace the cake flour with 1 cup plus
1 tablespoon plus 1 teaspoon (170 g)
gluten-free flour blend.

〰〰 **SEA LEVEL** 〰〰

Bake at 350°F for 30 minutes, or until a
toothpick inserted in the center comes
out clean.

Preheat the oven to 350°F. Line two 6-inch cake pans with parchment paper.

To make the batter: In the bowl of a stand mixer fitted with the paddle attachment, add the ½ cup butter, cane sugar, and almond extract. Mix on low until combined and no chunks of butter remain. Add the eggs, milk, and coconut milk and mix on low until combined.

In a separate bowl, add the cake flour, baking powder, cardamom, and sea salt and whisk together. With the mixer on low, slowly add the flour to the butter mixture and continue to mix on low until combined into a smooth batter, scraping down the sides of the bowl as needed.

Divide the batter evenly into the prepared cake pans, about 11 ounces (318 grams) each. Bake for 25 minutes, or until a toothpick inserted in the center comes out clean. Allow to cool completely before removing.

To make the frosting: In the bowl of a stand mixer fitted with the paddle attachment, add the ¾ cup butter, powdered sugar, and vanilla extract. Mix on low until combined and then speed up the mixer to high for 1 minute more, or until light and fluffy.

Place the first cake layer on a cake stand or spinner, place a generous amount of frosting onto the cake layer. Top with the second cake layer and frost the outside of the cake with the remaining frosting.

Immediately, completely cover the frosting with the fine shredded coconut; you must do this right away before the frosting starts to dry so it will stick.

Store in an airtight container or a cake dome for up to 3 days.

Carrot Cake

Makes a three-layer 6-inch cake

Carrot cake was one of the very first cake recipes I created. So naturally it was the first cake we added to the menu at Dessert'D. I created this recipe inside my tiny white beachside kitchen when I lived in Southern California. I later spent time crafting and perfecting it when my husband, Delaney, and I were first dating, and I wanted to impress him with a birthday cake. Ultimately a success, this recipe became the cake he requested for his birthday every year. It started out as a cake I made by hand, although you can use a stand mixer with a paddle attachment if you prefer. It is such a good recipe that even after so many years it has barely changed at all! — MIMI

BATTER

1⅓ cups (170 g) all-purpose flour

⅓ cup (30 g) unsweetened finely shredded coconut

1 teaspoon cinnamon

¾ teaspoon baking powder

½ teaspoon fine sea salt

6 ounces (170 g) carrots, finely grated

1 cup (226 g) cane sugar

½ cup (120 ml) canola oil

2 large eggs

FROSTING

¾ cup (170 grams) salted butter, softened

Heaping 2⅓ cups (340 g) powdered sugar, sifted

1 teaspoon vanilla extract

TOPPING

1 tablespoon (14 g) cane sugar

1 teaspoon cinnamon

············· GLUTEN-FREE ·············

Replace the all-purpose flour with 1 cup plus 1 tablespoon plus 1 teaspoon (170 g) gluten-free flour blend.

〰〰〰 SEA LEVEL 〰〰〰

Bake at 350°F for 20 minutes, or until a toothpick inserted in th center comes out clean.

Preheat the oven to 350°F. Line three 6-inch cake pans with parchment paper.

To make the batter: In a medium bowl, add the flour, coconut, cinnamon, baking powder, and sea salt and whisk together. Set aside.

Add the carrots, 1 cup cane sugar, canola oil, and eggs to a large mixing bowl. Whisk until combined and the yolks are broken up. Add the flour mixture to the carrot mixture and whisk until a batter forms and no bits of flour remain.

Measure the batter evenly into each pan, about 8 ounces (226 g) each. Bake for 17 minutes, or until a toothpick inserted in the center comes out clean. Allow to cool completely before removing.

To make the frosting: In the bowl of a stand mixer fitted with the paddle attachment, add the butter, powdered sugar, and vanilla extract. Mix on low until the ingredients are combined, then speed up the mixer to high for 1 minute more, or until light and fluffy.

On a cake stand or spinner, place the first cake layer. Using a cake spatula place a generous amount of frosting and spread evenly. Place the second cake layer on top and repeat this process. Place the last cake layer and frost the cake with the remaining frosting.

To make the topping: In a small dish, mix together the 1 tablespoon cane sugar and 1 teaspoon cinnamon. Sprinkle on top of the finished cake.

Store in an airtight container or a cake dome for up to 3 days.

ACKNOWLEDGMENTS

Mimi: Thank you, Kimmy, for joining forces with me to create this amazing book. I am so happy you chose to say yes to my proposal to write it with me. You are the mountain and I am the baker, and together we have created something beautiful, adventurous, and delicious.

Thank you to my amazing husband, Delaney, for sticking his head in the kitchen and helping us recipe test, taste test, and chime in with ideas.

Clare Pelino, we wouldn't be here without you and all your hard work. Thank you! You truly are the best agent and friend I could ask for. I love that you saw my vision for this book before *any* of us even knew exactly what it would become. But you and I knew we had something for years before it manifested into this. I am so grateful for your constant support and guidance. I knew in my heart when we met that we would create more than one book together and I even voiced it to you—and now I can say it is true. I cannot wait to create many more!

Thank you, Ann Treistman and The Countryman Press, for seeing the potential in this book and choosing to publish it. And thank you to everyone behind the scenes at The Countryman Press for all that you do to put this book out into the world so people can bake, cook, and be inspired by the mountains.

Thank you to my parents for encouraging me to play outside at all costs—rain, snow, mud, and all. I wouldn't be living in Mammoth Lakes if it weren't for your constant support of skiing, snowboarding, and the overall outdoors.

Thank you to all our customers at Dessert'D Organic Bake shop who support our small mountain town bake shop.

Kimmy: I'm forever grateful for Mimi and her vision for bringing Dessert'D Organic Bake Shop to life. Because of her, we have the opportunity to write this book; she has inspired me to step outside my comfort zone and explore different ways of preparing food. Additionally, her beautiful photography and attention to detail makes this book a visual and taste bud masterpiece.

Thank you to my wonderful husband, Chris Benchetler, who has humored me by eating everything I have ever made him and has encouraged and supported me throughout my developing passion for cooking.

Thank you to Ann Treistman, The Countryman Press, and Clare Pelino for believing in us and our desire to create a heart-full book of recipes from the mountains.

I'm eternally grateful to my late mother, Judy Fasani, who taught me the importance of a well-balanced diet at an early age, and who also showed me how to make high-quality meals in under 30 minutes. I greatly appreciate my godfather, Danny Goeschl, for taking me on "father-daughter" dinner dates to fine dining restaurants. Those experiences, combined with his wisdom of culinary art and food preparation, taught me how food can be a passion and experience. I would have never fine-tuned my cooking skills without the guidance of my mother-in-law, Kathy Benchetler, who prepared countless meals for a household of hungry teenagers, and who always let me be part of her process in the kitchen.

I want to honor all the other friends, chefs, and food authors out there who have provided inspiration and creativity for my desire to cook. Lastly, thank you to everyone I have ever had the honor of making a meal for—because of you, my passion for cooking has grown roots.

VEGAN & GLUTEN-FREE RECIPE LIST

INDEX

Italics are used for illustrations.

ABOUT THE AUTHORS

Mimi Council has made a name for herself by developing all of her recipes to be made at high altitude or at sea level with just one simple adjustment. Mimi is an editor at *The FeedFeed*, where she curates the High-Altitude Baking Feed within the food community. Mimi and her desserts have been featured in *Shape* magazine and on the websites of *The FeedFeed*, Organic Valley, Green Wedding Shoes, 100 Layer Cake, and The Nest, among others.

Kimmy Fasani is a progressive leader in women's snowboarding and is the founder of Amusement Mountain. She has been featured on Outside TV, in the magazines S*nowboarder, Transworld* *Snowboarding*, and *Outside*, and on the websites of ESPN and *Teen Vogue*, as well as in popular snowboard films. Her passion for cooking has grown alongside her career as an athlete, always needing to refuel in high-elevation terrain.

Mimi and Kimmy live and bake in Mammoth Lakes, California, where they opened Dessert'D Organic Bake Shop in September 2011. It's been growing ever since. They are both self-taught bakers and cooks. Follow them at:
@mimibakescookies
@kimmyfasani
@dessertdorganic
www.dessertd.com